Joyce Thornton

TALKING ABOUT SOMETHING IMPORTANT

© Copyright 1981, Stan Stewart and Pauline Hubner

Published by The Joint Board of Christian Education of Australia and New Zealand, 177 Collins Street, Melbourne, Victoria 3000.

Design: Patrick Dowling, John Wilkins.

Cover: John Blomfield.

ISBN 0 85819 328 0

Talking about something important

by Stan Stewart and Pauline Hubner

THE JOINT BOARD OF
CHRISTIAN EDUCATION OF AUSTRALIA
AND NEW ZEALAND
Melbourne

Contents

Preface	5
Introduction	9
Chapter 1 　The evolution of a philosophy.	11
Chapter 2 　Talking about starting new things.	25
Chapter 3 　Talking about terrible news.	31
Chapter 4 　Talking about surprises and presents.	37
Chapter 5 　Talking about precious things.	45
Chapter 6 　Talking about the death of someone important.	57
Chapter 7 　Talking about the worst journey in the world.	67
Chapter 8 　Talking about my first song.	74
Chapter 9 　Talking about 'rude is . . . '	82
Chapter 10 　Talking about who makes wars.	89
Chapter 11 　Talking about a day for giving away treasure.	96
Chapter 12 　Talking about when people go away.	104
Chapter 13 　Talking about feeling quiet.	112
Chapter 14 　Principles to go with.	123
About the authors	127

Preface

'But where can we find good childrens addresses?' Whether in Australia, New Zealand or the United States, this is the question which will inevitably be asked by worship planners. Four years of leading workshops on childrens ministry has taught us that the search for an answer to this question motivates a considerable proportion of our workshop participants to attend.

To folk with this agenda, it comes as a surprise to realise that the childrens address is not one of the things we are greatly concerned about. Many have presumed that when we stress the need to involve children in worship, we must be talking about brighter and better childrens sermons. These folk are doubly surprised when they realise that, in our view, a childrens address is not an essential ingredient in forms of worship appropriate for children.

The inclusion of a childrens address is only one option for the congregation wanting to include their children in worship. Although this option has been taken up by so many protestant and episcopalian churches, this should not be seen as a warrant that it must now be a part of every Sunday morning liturgy.

The fact is that the childrens address is a modern invention. For centuries, generations of children have been involved in and related to liturgies which have lacked anything which resembles the modern childrens address.

Nor should it be concluded that the presence of a childrens address means that this congregation welcomes children in worship; quite the opposite is frequently the truth. The childrens address has often been used as a sop to humour the children in what is basically a very anti-children gathering. All too easily, the childrens address becomes a way of patting children on the heads whilst at the same time shooing them out the door, either literally out the church door, or psychologically, by closing for them the door of interest and meaning from that point onwards in the liturgy.

But, despite its weaknesses, the childrens address is not about to go away. As many ministers can testify, any suggestion of dropping the childrens address will be met by loud objections. This emotive protest will come not from the children, but from the adults; in the matter of childrens addresses, most usually the children have no say. Adult congregations will suffer many things from their worship leaders, but not the elimination of the childrens address.

When inquiring why this is so, an answer often given is: 'It's the only part of the service I can understand'. Whilst shuddering to think what this says about the rest of the worship service, we also find ourselves doubting if this is the true reason, and if our hunch is correct, the question remains: 'For adults, what is the appeal of the childrens address?'

One of the things adults seem to look for in a childrens address is something to make them laugh. Most ministers do what they can to oblige. To the congregation, it seems to matter little where the laugh lines come from. They may be on or off the subject, against the presenter, or, as too frequently happens, at the expense of the children.

It is observable that most ministers use a different style of communication in the childrens address than in the rest of the service. This sometimes means a different tone of voice and it always means more informality. Despite what adults may say about the meaning they find in the childrens addresses, we suspect that it is the unbending of their ministers which they most enjoy.

No doubt, the children also enjoy the more relaxed presentation of their minister, but probably they enjoy it less than the adults. As for the funny stories or asides, they are usually above their heads.

It is against this background that we write this book. We belong to a denomination in which the childrens address has been institutionalised in most churches. We recognise that, for good or ill, it will continue to be part of the worship patterns of most congregations for the foreseeable future. Despite the views expressed by many regarding the value of the childrens address, it is our opinion that it often constitutes an unhelpful intrusion into the worship service. This happens when it detracts from the wholeness of worship for all ages in the congregation. We are convinced that this need not be so.

In this book, we provide an approach to the childrens segment which enables it to contribute to worship in two significant ways. First, it ensures that the childrens part of worship *means* something to the children; secondly, it *relates* the childrens segment to the worship and vice versa. In this way, the childrens segment contributes to the wholeness of worship and not to its detraction.

In this book, we share an approach which has worked for us in achieving these aims. It is not the only approach we use, but it is the approach to which we return most frequently. The twelve chapters are variations on a way of talking with children about things which are not only important to them, but have meaning for the entire congregation. In each chapter, one of us retells how a specific theme was developed in a particular worship service. In some cases, the setting for this service was unusual; but, in no case was the setting unique. On the contrary, the twelve themes dealt with in this book recur often throughout life. They are universals which keep popping up in the lives of children and which, just as surely, are part of life for adults too.

Originally, it was our intention to include with each chapter a *How to do it* section. In the process of writing the book, we decided against this. The more we wrote, the more we realised just how individual was our approach. At the same time, it became clear that this was not a bad thing. We came to see that our willingness to risk and be ourselves was the real reason which made these segments tick, and we decided that whatever we wrote would, above all, encourage readers to do the same. In other areas of childrens work, we have seen examples of how a set of suggestions has become an inflexible rubric. When this has happened, something of the humanity and spontaneity of the presenter has been lost.

The 'talking about something important' approach works best in an atmosphere of interpersonal honesty, and with leaders who can live comfortably with an open-ended situation. This being the case, it seems quite unwise to set out steps which must be followed or to detail precisely how each topic should be developed. The nature of the interchange will always depend on the persons involved — who they are and where they are coming from. Considerations like these made us feel that a *How to do it* section might prove to be more of a distraction than a help.

The approach we finally adopted was to set out information on four levels. At the beginning and the close of the book, we have attempted to establish our evolving philosophy and the principles which form the guidelines we usually follow. Part one of each chapter tells the story of what happened during the childrens address portion of a particular worship service. In part two of these chapters, we give details about the context of that particular worship service together with any personal factors which influenced our preparation of it. The chapters conclude with explanations and examples of how the childrens section related to the whole liturgy, and vice versa.

On topics where readers' personal experience makes them at ease with the way we introduced a theme, there is no reason why they should not follow our approach in its entirety. However, we suspect that in most cases, folk will want to adapt and alter routines to fit in with local circumstances and their own personal style. And when talking about something important with children, this is the way it should always be. In this sharing of our approach to the twelve life themes, we hope we are pointing a direction, and not detailing a precise route. Your children and your church will gain most from your leadership when you have them walk in these directions according to your feelings, and at your pace.

Introduction

This book is built around twelve true stories. The setting for each account is the same. It is what is usually known in protestant and anglican worship as the time of the childrens address. This four to seven minute segment placed early in the liturgy is the time in which the minister or some worship leader talks to the children. All of the services from which the stories in this book are taken were led by either one of us; they took place in a variety of churches across Australia.

The stories are based on some of our expreriences of talking with children in church. But as we tell them in this book, these stories are not for reading to children. Rather they are set out here to be pondered by story tellers, worship leaders and anyone who has an interest in, or responsibility for, communicating with children. All of this is not to say that the stories will be devoid of interest to children. Certainly, that is not so. But our intention is that our stories and the topics they raise be mixed into the experience of our readers and the children with whom they wish to communicate. We believe that it will only be through some process like this that they will become for others, the valued communication pieces they have been for us.

It would be a mistake to think that this is a book of childrens sermons. It would be equally far from the mark to think that this book is about how to deliver better childrens addresses. The truth is that this book is about another way of using the time allotted for the childrens address than to address children. The 'talking about something important approach' we advocate is something quite different.

The restraints of time and of the formal church setting means that the childrens segment in worship has always tended to be a contrived affair. Despite all of this, it has a number of communication possibilities; talking to children is only one of these. The approach illustrated by the stories in this book places central importance on talking with children.

There is nothing new under the sun and we are aware that children have been answering questions in church for years. This is fine as far as it goes, but something more is needed. The 'talking with children' to which we refer in this book is talking with children about their experience of life and the questions it raises for them. When adults talk to children in church, it is always about something important. But usually the 'something important' has been chosen by the adults. It is something which the adult presenter feels should be important to the children, whether they like it or not. The 'something important' that we refer to in the title of this book, is something which children know to be important to them. We believe our twelve stories illustrate how simply this can be done. The stories also illustrate that what is important to children will also be important to the entire congregation. When this is realised, the childrens segment becomes something other than a story interlude inserted for the sake of the kids, an interlude which, apart from providing a little light relief, has no relevance to any other part of the worship. Instead, the childrens segment becomes an important resource which can be drawn upon in the prayers, meditation and preaching of that day's worship.

Despite its primary focus on children in church, this book is not only for ministers and worship leaders. The reason being, that talking with children about something important to them should be the concern of everyone who in the name of Jesus wants to communicate with children. The examples given in this book all took place in the confined environment of a worship service, but the approach can be even more effective in a less formal setting. Here, then, is another way of approaching devotional segments in a childrens club or teacher/pupil interaction in a Sunday school class. Perhaps the most important forum for talking with children about something important is in the home. Parents, grandparents and all friends of children should be aware of this. From time to time, the children in their lives will crave the opportunity to talk with adults close to them about something which they feel to be important.

Chapter 1

The evolution of a philosophy

Everybody does not love Saturday nights!

Early in my ministry, there was a song on the hit parade which used to annoy me immensely. It went 'Everybody loves Saturday nights'. With slight variation, this lyric was repeated throughout the length of the song. The reason for my dislike of the song was basic. I did not like Saturday nights. For me, Saturday night was the dreariest night of the week. I had one chore which made it that way. That unwelcome task was searching for a childrens address.

During the week, I would prepare my sermon and prayers. But like a trip to the dentist, finding a childrens address was something I always put off. Then with Saturday night came the realisation that the task could be postponed no longer. Yuk . . .

To me, the childrens address was the least important part of the service. My ministerial training had confirmed in me the correctness of this valuation. Frankly, I wished I could leave it out. I knew that this would cause more fuss than it was worth, which was infuriating because it was the adults who were the enthusiasts for the childrens address. As far as I could judge, the children were totally apathetic about the whole thing.

The Saturday night prowl through my bookshelves became an unpleasant ritual; unpleasant because it was generally so fruitless. The object of my search was a story with a high moral tone which contained at least an element of adventure, and hopefully with a funny twist somewhere. It was desirable that the tale conclude with a Christian exhortation.

This latter bit, however, was not an essential criterion, as I found that I could always tack it on. My shelves were not short of books which claimed to be crammed with suitable stories for my childrens address needs. After poring through their pages, I often felt that some authors ought to be sued for deceptive advertising. In a couple of the quite large books, I was unable to find one single story I could use. Even the better books had no more than three or four stories which I could happily manage to retell.

I can well remember the desperation of those Saturday nights. Again and again, I would look at the stories I had previously rejected, my last ditch hope being to find some way to modify one of them so that I could tell it with a modicum of enthusiasm. By dint of perseverance and mighty ingenuity, I always managed to find a story. Even so, on most Saturday nights I left the study dissatisfied, vowing to continue my search for better resource books. Each time I went to the Christian book store, my heart would quicken. I would think, 'Perhaps today I will find the book from which I can tell all of the stories'. It never happened.

THERE HAS TO BE SOMETHING BETTER

Visiting preachers used to irritate me. They always had such fantastic childrens addresses. Later, when I was frequently a visiting preacher myself, I woke up to the secret of their success. Visiting preachers only need one or two childrens addresses. As they move from place to place, they can repeat the same story endlessly. Once a visiting preacher came across a childrens address which made the adults laugh and interested the children, they stuck to it. From then on, it was a perennial part of their repertoire. As a visiting preacher myself, I quickly learned to do the same. I still have two sure-fire childrens addresses which I can deliver without notice, whether I am awake or asleep. Knowing the secret of the visiting preachers made me feel a little better about myself. When it came to childrens addresses, I was not the world's greatest dummy after all. But that still did not help me with my week-by-week commitment in my local parish.

According to the books on the subject, it seems that the best source of childrens addresses are object lessons. Having some object to show the children is the way to gain undivided attention. So went the theory, and I must confess that usually it worked, at least for a couple of minutes. I found that holding up the object was the easy part. The tricky bit was drawing from the object a spiritual lesson. Some were most predictable; a shiny apple with a diseased centre, for instance, spoke directly of looking good but being bad (sinful) inside. Others required an imaginative flair of genius to make the connection, like the man I once saw puffing flour out of a trumpet. The spiritual message in this action always eluded me, but I never will forget the spectacle he created as the cloud of flour fell softly around the pulpit.

True adventure stories have always been in vogue for childrens addresses. Usually these stories were about admirable figures in the past, generally the distant past. It is my impression that the social standing of the congregation had considerable bearing on the type of people exemplified in these stories. For instance, I noticed that hard line evangelicals had a preference for telling stories from the lives of evangelists. On the other hand, ministers of upper crust and educated congregations tended to tell incidents from the lives of literary figures, playwrights and famous politicians. The run of the mill congregations mostly heard about sportsmen and Christian pioneers. I noticed that the one thing most of these adventure stories had in common, was that the central figures were long dead. I can still remember childrens addresses from my childhood about sportsmen of the last century, proving their Christian commitment by steadfastly refusing to bow to pressure to play sport on Sundays.

Adventure stories to suit all types of congregations continue to be printed. These days, their covers are brighter. Nonetheless, it is my impression that they still draw their stories from the golden age of childrens addresses, which was about 100 years ago.

Personally, I preferred 'little Johnny' tales. I was introduced to these stories by a Methodist lay preacher, who was a school teacher by trade. He had an endless supply of stories about children. He swore that they were all true but, to protect the innocent in every story, he called the hero or villain, as may have been the case, 'little Johnny'. Little Johnny caught my imagination, and in my own search for a childrens address, I often thought of him. On a few occasions, I used the pseudonym to conceal my own identity as I retold a childhood escapade. When absolutely desperate, I must confess to making up little Johnny stories to suit my purpose. When telling them, I eased my conscience by the thought that something like this probably did happen to some child, somewhere, sometime.

When it came to supplying regular, fascinating childrens addresses, the people who, to my mind, had it made were people who were skilled at instant sketching. Green with envy, I have watched colleagues bring a story to life through well chosen lines.

Lacking this talent, I have tried on several occasions to prepare on a blackboard or butchers paper some sketches and, by slight of hand, to reveal them at the appropriate moment. I was never able to use this method to my satisfaction.

On several occasions, I became so involved with the mechanics that I lost my grip on the story. I played with the idea of buying a flannelgraph, but abandoned this idea in the belief that my problems with this medium would be even worse.

After ten years of ministry, I seemed to have tried everything, but I was not feeling any better about the childrens address. Nothing worked, at least not consistently.

I doubt if my congregations would have shared this view. My childrens addresses were not inferior to those of other worship leaders and not infrequently, they were little better than average. But in my heart, I felt I was walking a treadmill. I doubted if this segment of worship was making much sense to the children and I felt sure it was contributing little to the worship service.

In 1975, I began a research task for the Australian Council of Christian Education which had as its focus children in the local parish. For months, I seemed to eat, sleep and dream children in church. It was at this point that my grumble of discontent became a giant of frustration. My dissatisfaction with the job I was doing with the childrens address increased dramatically. 'Surely', I thought, 'there must be a better way to use this time'.

STUMBLING INTO MEANING

Once or twice a year, I use a film to replace the sermon. On the occasion I am about to describe, I had chosen a first-rate audio-visual. The audio-visual dealt with the inner dynamics of personal faith. It approached this subject in a sophisticated manner using symbols, allegory and clever scripting. For adults and young people, it was excellent. It had an open-ended conclusion which begged for discussion.

There was no way that children could understand the images or the subtleties of this presentation, but that did not worry me at all since the children were scheduled to go to the crèche. However, on this occasion, they noticed the audio-visual equipment in the aisle of the church, and when I announced it was time for them to leave for crèche, I sensed that some were reluctant to go. I gathered that the children felt that anything with projected pictures would be interesting to them. On the spur of the moment, I said that any children who wanted to stay for the presentation could do so. In doing this, I was careful to point out that the audio-visual had been made for adults and that they would have a hard job understanding it. Undeterred, over half of the children stayed.

Throughout the showing of the film-strip, I was wondering whatever I could do with the children at the conclusion of the screening. Certainly, they could not join in the adult discussion. As I looked at them, their young faces seemed to be taking it all in. 'Taking what in?' was the question in my mind.

By the end of the film-strip, I had decided that the only possible solution would be to have the children join me at the front of the church. I set the adults to discussing the film-strip with folk seated around them. They were immediately engrossed in grappling with the questions raised by the film. The children had gladly gathered around me. Their expectant faces were clearly asking, 'What next?'. So was I.

I had already used my childrens address for the day and no other suitable inspirational titbit came to my mind. Lacking anything else, I asked, 'What did you think the film-strip was all about?' From my point of view, this was a stall which I hoped would give me a minute or so to think of something to tell them. I was not ready for the children's response. Several children immediately had an answer to my question. One after the other, they gave their explanation of the presentation. Their explanations bore no relationship to an adult's perception of the film-strip. Starting from the image which had meaning to them, each child developed a scenario about the message of the film. The interpretations were all different, but to me, the astounding thing was that each interpretation made a kind of sense. No one laughed. Nor did I. Nor should we have, because no one was being silly.

The time for discussion was over before all of the children had had their say. Moved by the seriousness with which the children took their task, I asked two of them to start the plenary session with their explanation of what the strip was all about. As the children talked, the rest of the congregation smiled broadly. The children took the smiles to be affirmation and felt good about their contributions. The children then respectfully listened to the adult contributions which must have been as surprising to them as theirs was to the adults.

Walking home from church that Sunday morning, I tried to work through what had happened. The least one could say was that the children were happily with us through a worship service which had been ninety minutes in duration. That in itself was surprising, but my mind was exercised by some things which were even more unexpected. I tried to recapture inwardly those moments of panic when I sat before the children with nothing to say. Why was I so frightened?

In the event, it was all so unnecessary. The answer was simple enough: I had been conditioned to think that in church, ministers talked to children. They told them things about God and how to grow to be a good Christian. No other communication pattern was appropriate or possible. The experience of the morning had shaken this assumption.

To me, the most amazing thing was that each child had found in the audio-visual some serious meaning. Although their perceptions were quite different to mine, I was inspired by their interpretations. On other occasions when I had asked children for contributions in church, it was always in response to some input I had fed them. It was like a teacher quizzing a class to see if they had been listening. This morning's circumstances had forced me to go to the children empty-handed and ask their opinion on a subject I had not primed. Now I had to recognise that out of their young mouths had come insight which I had not given them.

Although I did not immediately recognise it, the incident had challenged my whole approach to the childrens segment in worship. Despite what educators said about not ending a childrens address with a moral, I knew that most people did. And so did I. It did not seem right to leave the childrens address without spelling out its meaning. Further to this, some of the stories and object lessons I had used would make not the slightest bit of sense without the spiritual ending. It became the validation for what otherwise could have been a diversion with no relationship to the rest of the worship hour.

On that morning, there was no way in which I could neatly wrap up the childrens comments. They had to stand as they were. If they made sense, they made sense, but if they did not, then too bad. But it was not too bad. It did not detract from the meaning of the occasion; in fact, it probably added to it. I began to wonder if I had stumbled onto another way of approaching children in church. Not just talking *to* children but talking *with* them. Not telling them answers, but looking together at questions. Here is one of the seeds from which the concept of talking about something important grew in me.

FIT FOR WORSHIP

I was intrigued by the possibility of using the childrens address time to ask children questions about serious things. What I was unsure about was just what subjects would be suitable for this kind of in-church dialogue. It was my readings in the book of Psalms which more than anything else helped me with this question. As a young person, it was my impression that the Psalms were all about praising God. When I began to study the Psalms, it soon became clear that this was not the case. A significant portion of the Psalms are never used in liturgies and seldom appear in devotional readings. These little-used verses took up many themes other than praise and joy. Doubting, crying, shouting, cursing, hurting, despairing and grieving all find expression in this royal treasury of ancient hymns. The songs of this book give expression to the entire range of human emotions. To me, the most helpful thing was the realisation that the Psalms place the hardest questions of life and the darkest side of human emotions alongside the paeans of praise. Within the one Psalm, there can be the starkest of contrasts between faith and doubt, praise and complaint (for example, Psalm 27 in the *Jerusalem Bible*). And yet, as often as not, no attempt is made to deal with the contradictions. The Book of Psalms is definitely not a book of tidy endings. Although praise of God and trust in God are the dominant themes of the book, its poems are shot through with unanswered questions and matters pending.

Out of this convergence of ideas and experiences, I began to have second thoughts about subjects which could be appropriate for a childrens address. The Psalms had shown me that the whole of life with all its questions and emotions were matters to be brought before God. 'Why not, then', I reasoned, 'use the childrens address to talk with the children about *any* matters which were of serious concern to them?'

Previously, I had steered away from subjects unless I had a definite answer to any questions which the children might raise. Along with many other ministers and teachers, I felt that to stand before children without answers was to stand naked. This attitude constantly placed me in a dilemma. On the one hand, I would frequently find myself spouting clichés which deep down I knew were inadequate; on the other hand, a lack of formula answers meant I left whole slices of life without any mention at all.

It was a combination of discontent with this situation, my experience with the children and the audio-visual, and my reflection on the Psalms that made me determined to try to break this deadlock. If, I reasoned, it was appropriate in the context of worship to raise questions and to leave them unresolved, then I could avoid both horns of the problem. This in turn meant that open-ended discussion or comment on any life experience was material fit for inclusion in a worship service.

The conviction grew within me that such an approach would really help the children to understand the Christian faith. After all, it is not just the Psalms that lack formula answers; the whole Bible is full of unanswered questions and unresolved issues. The traditional childrens address hardly, if ever, reflected this dimension of faith. Year in, year out, the childrens part of the service was given over to addresses which neatly concluded with a moral and a spiritual version of a 'happily ever after' ending. Life is not like that, not even the Christian life. Raising hard questions, talking about them, praying about them and leaving them unresolved before God is often the Bible's way. So it was that I felt emboldened to try a similar approach, believing it would more realistically depict the faith we sought to commend to our children.

There was another idea which flickered in my mind. I had already felt moved by the children's wisdom in the face of an inexplicable film. 'Perhaps', I thought, 'the children might have some insights into the hard questions which will help us all'. Later experience would prove this hunch to be true.

INTERRUPTIONS WITH SPECIAL INTEREST OR CONTRIBUTIONS TO WHOLENESS

In the churches of my childhood, items were thought to be high points of worship. We used to have items of all kinds; musical items were the most frequent. The congregations of my early years were too small to have a regular choir, so our music came mostly from soloists. The other times I can most clearly remember were recitations. These would be poems on spiritual subjects, or Bible verses which had been committed to memory. Whenever we had an item, it was introduced grandly and followed by words of appreciation. However, the item seldom had any relationship to the rest of the worship service. It seems to me that both then and now, items of this sort are interruptions with special interest and little relevance.

The twig goes the way it is bent, and so in the early years of my ministry, items had a place in worship whenever we could get them. Thinking back, I have come to realise that the only regular item we had was my childrens address. Some may be surprised to hear mention of the childrens address as an item. But, in my view, that is what it was. It has all the hallmarks of an item. Congregations look for childrens addresses which have in them elements of drama or comedy or pathos, and preferably all three. The spiritual content is important but no more important than the entertainment which surrounds it. As with an item, there is no necessity that the address be related to the rest of the worship service in any way. That is, the childrens address is an interruption with special interest and no particular relevance. To folk raised to expect items in worship, this all seems fine, and so it did to me, until I began to think that the childrens address could mean more.

When I began to experiment with talking about life issues with children, I soon realised that the topics were also life issues for adults. Unlike the prosaic little stories with their neat endings, these life matters touched the entire congregation. This being the case, once an issue had been raised, it was not only the children who needed some way of responding to them. I began to extend the consideration of the matter discussed with children into the rest of the service. As this happened, I became aware that the childrens address was becoming more than an item. It was developing into a resource with relevance to the whole of the worship event. As much as I had previously liked items, I realised that here was something greatly to be preferred.

The Psalms had taught me that the worship of God can hold in its compass contradictory aspects of life and faith. This same book taught me that these contradictions need not be disconnected entities. Each component of worship can and should contribute in some way to the rest of the service. Reflecting on an aspect of life with the children and then relating to it in other parts of the service became to me a most powerful worship experience. From then on, I deliberately worked at making the childrens segment relate to the worship of that day. On occasions, the theme of the childrens segment pointed a direction to follow through the ensuing worship. More frequently, I worked backwards from the lectionary theme for that day to the childrens segment. Whichever approach I used, it was soon quite plain to everyone that the childrens address was not an isolated item. As this happened, the entire worship service made more sense to everyone, young and old.

A SPECIAL KIND OF DIALOGUE FOR A VERY SPECIAL PLACE.

Meaningful talk with children in the atmosphere of a formal church service may seem to many like an impossible dream. A rationale for this point of view is not hard to find. The physical arrangement of many sanctuaries makes it well-nigh impossible for the person out front to talk with anyone, let alone people who are three feet high and under. Then, there is a bunch of problems which relate to communicating with children. For instance, there is the problem of uncommunicative children. By temperament, some children never have much to say. What hope is there of talking with children in church if you happen to strike a situation in which there are a number of children with this temperament? Just as bad is the situation in which one talkative child wants to answer everything! Any of these situations would have daunted me. That is, until I came to realise that there are other ways of talking with children than having children talk out loud. Just as some dialogues can be so manipulated as to take on all the characteristics of a monologue, so some monologues can in fact create the response dialogue.

The person who taught me most about talking with children is a person who normally never talks with children; the reason being that he is host of a childrens television program. All of his professional contact with children is via the television tube. His medium is one-way communication, but he is by no means a one-way communicator. Fred Rogers is a Presbyterian minister who has been ordained to a ministry to families through the electronic media. For years, he has exercised this ministry across America through a television program for pre-school children titled *Mr Rogers' Neighbourhood*.

The first time I saw the program, I thought it was possibly the slowest and almost certainly, the most boring program I had ever seen. I presumed that my viewing companion, a four year old child, was as bored as I was. But part-way into the program, the hitherto silent child began to speak. At first, I thought he was speaking to me. When I saw that this was not the case, I thought he must have been talking to himself. On the third try, I got it right; he was talking to the man on the television! As strange as it first seemed, this child was having a conversation with the man on the television program. Looking back at the program, I realised that this man was not talking *to* children, he was talking *with* them. I now know that this gentle man is in regular communication with millions of children.

Talking with children 'Mr Rogers style' means raising issues which children know about from their own life experience. It means talking about these things in a friendly but serious way. It means starting where the children are, and helping them to articulate their fears, and to be at ease with their feelings. And most of all, it means giving unambiguous signs that you are interested in the children and in their world.

Mr Rogers' way of talking with children does not depend on the children being able to talk back to him. It depends rather on his willingness to enter respectfully into the childrens world in an attitude of personal honesty. When this is done, the conditions for dialogue are present. The dialogue Mr Rogers commences through the one-way medium of television is continued by his child viewers in their minds, with their parents, with teachers and with friends. It is also worth noting that something similar to this happens with the adult viewers to a program.

As I began to explore the possibility of having conversations with children in church, Mr Rogers provided me with a model. I was well aware that an out loud, one-to-one conversation with all the children in church was not a possibility. But Fred Rogers helped me see that it was possible to commence an inner dialogue with many of the children. I saw that this was possible when children sensed that (a) I was talking *with* them and not *to* them; and (b) I was sincerely trying to address myself to their life experience and the questions it was throwing up for them.

Most times, I was able to ensure that some children had the opportunity to respond out loud in the church service. But, usually the constraint of time would mean that only a few children could speak. On some occasions, I used a small group approach which gave all the children a chance to speak with the people sitting around them. The effectiveness of these occasions depended to a large extent on the ability of the adults to relate to the children. For most children on most occasions, the dialogue went on in their heads. At times, it was continued on the way home or at home. I heard of some occasions when children referred to something we had talked about, months after we had raised it in church. This was something which never happened after my childrens addresses, not even the best of them. Whether standing behind or in front of a lectern, with children around me or still sitting in the pews, I found that I was able to talk with children. I now believe that when children sense that you are talking with them, you see the dialogue going on. You can see it in their eyes.

DECIDING WHAT IS IMPORTANT

Who decides when there is something important to talk about? In the stories which follow, it will be seen that it has been the adult leaders who have done most of the deciding. At times, we have felt that church, or a community event, or a matter of world news has pushed a topic upon us. The possibility of the children themselves nominating the important thing to be discussed is certainly there, but as yet we have not taken it up. Children and especially small children, though they are aware of their needs, often cannot articulate them. They will, therefore, respond with warmth and gratitude to adults who attempt to understand their needs and to talk to them.

A FRESH START FOR OLD WAYS

The 'Talking About Something Important' approach has completely changed the childrens segment in the services I lead. Since starting on this track, I have never again opened the covers of my books of childrens sermons. This is not because I use the ways set out in this book every Sunday; I don't. In fact, about once a month, I use a fairly standard childrens address format. However, from my perspective, even this is now quite different.

These days, when looking for a childrens address, I search not my bookshelves, but my life and the lives of children known to me. I draw inspiration from three strands. One is my own recent experience. What has happened to me during this past week? The second is what has come to me through my recent contact with children. What have they said and what have I noticed? The third is my own childhood. Is there anything from my memories which spoke to me and may speak to others? This trinity of resources has never let me down.

I have reason to believe that for the recipients of the childrens addresses, things are noticeably different in two ways. From the childrens point of view, I am always talking about something which they know is immediate to me and is generally not far from them. Perhaps the biggest difference for everyone is that the childrens address is no longer an isolated item. It belongs to the rest of the service. It relates positively to what precedes and follows it.

These days, there are many Sundays on which there is no childrens segment as such. On Sundays when the liturgy breaks out of its verbal straightjacket and moves into more lively forms of communication, it can be enough for children to be part of the congregation. As often as possible, the children participate in the leadership of worship. On special occasions, it is their contribution which adds the extra beauty and drama to the liturgy. As appropriate, they bring their facility for dance and art to enrich and enliven the worship for all ages. Sometimes, through action or art, the children are saying more than they know. The message they proclaim, they perceive in part only. That is as it has always been with the involvement of children in ceremonial life. It is enough for them to sense that they are involved in an action of great importance to the people of God, and that through their work, they are contributing to the praise of God.

These other forms of involvement of children in worship are a subject to be taken up elsewhere. What we share in this book is an approach that we have found to be central and formative in our own understanding of relating with children in worship. Through it, we have learned much about communicating with children and about the contribution they can bring to the worship of the congregation. In many ways, for us, talking with children about something important has been a flash by which both our understanding of worship and of children has been illuminated. And we hope readers will quickly see that talking about something important is not only for the kids. The implications of this approach are as important for adults as they are for children.

Chapter 2

Talking about starting new things

'Is there anyone here who this week started kindergarten for the first time?' Almost immediately, I heard the chatter of tiny voices. A number of small hands waved frantically in the air. 'Would the new kindergarten people like to come and join me at the front of the church?' I asked. For some, there was no hesitation. Others needed urging to move into the aisle. But once there, they came running. On that Sunday, seven little people gathered around the lectern. They had no idea what I wanted of them. They only knew that the minister was interested in kindergarten people. For each of them, starting kinder had been just about the biggest thing in their life so far.

In preparation for their coming, I had placed a long bench seat at the front of the church. This was not for them to sit on, but to stand on. Clambering up onto the form, they stood there facing the congregation. The sight of these beaming little people sent a ripple of pleasure through the congregation.

Roving microphone in hand, I addressed them: 'I would like to congratulate you all on commencing kinder'. They gladly accepted my congratulations for they all knew that this new beginning was no mean achievement. 'I'm sure that going to kinder must make you feel grown up.' They nodded their heads in agreement. 'I wonder would you mind sharing something of your first week in kinder?' Some looked apprehensive but most looked eager to try. 'What I thought to do', I said, 'was to ask some questions and if you know the answer, you may like to tell us'. Gesturing to the congregation, I told them, 'Just about everyone here today would love to hear something about how you got on in your first week in kinder'.

'Can any of you tell us the name of your teacher?' One hand shot up. I walked along the line with the microphone. I first asked the participant to tell the congregation his name, and then his teacher's name. Speaking into the microphone, the child's voice was clearly heard by all the congregation. One answer led to another and soon we knew their names and quite a few kindergarten instructors'.

My second question to them was: 'Tell me, what did you most enjoy about your week of kindergarten?' This time, a number of children were immediately eager to answer. They talked about painting, playing, eating, climbing, and listening to stories. For a moment it sounded as though kindergarten was a pleasure palace filled with happy children. I knew this was only half the story.

'Did any of you have any trouble or sad times at kinder this week?' On this occasion, there was a little hesitation. Then a small girl said she had a sad thing to tell. She told us of being pushed over and how hard it had been to stop crying. A boy then felt bold enough to tell us he felt upset when his mummy left him on the first day. A little girl talked about a child who wouldn't share. Some of the children had things to say which did not relate to any of the questions. Each of these comments was heard.

Throughout the interviews, I had tried through my demeanour and responses, to communicate two things to the children and the congregation: one, that the children were not before them to put on a comedy show; and, two, that their confidences were to be valued. Certainly, we laughed together. You can't talk with children without this happening. But I tried to avoid the impression that anyone was laughing at them.

I then directed the children's attention towards the congregation. I said, 'Boys and girls, you are not the only ones who this week started something new'. Addressing the congregation, I asked, 'Hands up any mother who for the first time in a long time, no longer has a child at home during the day'. The children and I could see a number of mothers with their hands up. Some children saw their own mothers with a hand in the air. As they lowered their hands, I said to the children, 'You know, it's a big thing for you to start kinder, but did you know it's a big thing for your mothers when you leave home to go to kinder? For some mothers it's a sad thing when their child goes off to kinder'. The children looked impressed. 'And', I added, 'some of them are glad, because now they have time to start some new things'.

Over the next couple of minutes, I used this same 'hands up' technique to discover more people who had recently started new things. As hands rose in response to specific questions, we all saw khat sitting in church that morning were folk who were starting many new things. Some had just started new jobs, quite a few were starting new studies, one family had just moved into a new house, and two people had recently retired from work. At no point did the children appear to lose interest. They seemed pleased that others were also willing to share their new beginnings. I told the children that these adults would be feeling most of the nervousness and excitement that they had felt in their first week of kinder.

Before the children climbed down, I led a prayer. My prayer went something like this:

'Lord, we pray for these children who this week have commenced kindergarten. We thank you for the new friends they have made, for the fun they are having and for the new things they are learning.

We ask that you will help them with the hard things they meet at kindergarten. Be with them when they feel lonely, when they are frightened or hurt. Lord, at these times, help them to find a friend and to know always that you love them.

Lord, forgive us when we hurt other people, when we won't share, when we push others around, when we get angry because we don't get our own way. Help us to stop being like this, and teach us to be a good friend to all we meet.

As we pray for these children, so we pray for everyone here today who is beginning something new.

We ask this prayer in the name of the one who is at the beginning of all things, Jesus Christ. Amen.'

THE SETTING

Once is enough for some of the special things we try in worship. They may be interesting but they do not bear repeating. On the other hand, there are some segments which just beg to be repeated. What is more, they seem to grow in power as they are proceeded with, again and again. Their innate meaning and significance is strengthened by repetition, and this is warrant enough to give such segments a regular place in the cycle of the congregation's year. A simple celebration of the first week of kinder is one such event.

This segment draws strength from two power sources which are constantly being renewed. One power source is the beauty of small children. This God-given gift can stir a gentle joyfulness in those who look at them. Neither young nor old can remain unmoved when small children stand before them. A second source is the way in which the children raise issues which are always present at each new stage of life. In talking about their first week at kinder, they bring to light in their most basic formulations, universals which are always present in growth and risking. This is to say that all ages know and have experienced the joys and anxieties of which the children speak.

A further reason for making this an annual event is that it provides an opportunity for a congregation to say to all its children: 'We are thinking of you as you grow up, and meet with new experiences'. There are many ways in which this can be done. To my mind, the best way is by directing attention on those who have just negotiated their first week in kinder. This judgment is based on the observation that, for most children, this step causes great excitement, and, for some, deep trauma.

Obviously, something similar could be done for those children who have just been through their first week at school, or who have just moved into high school. It has not been my practice to do this; rather, I am careful to mention children in these situations in my communications with the kinders. Practice seems to bear out my hunch that for most children, entry into kinder is the symbol *par excellence* of all new beginnings. In actual fact, the way in which I use it makes it a symbol of all new beginnings for all ages.

To sum up, this celebration takes place annually on the Sunday morning which follows the first week of kindergarten. The segment usually takes six to seven minutes, though on occasions it has taken ten minutes. The length of time depends largely on the talkativeness of the children.

RESOURCING WORSHIP

Matters related to 'newness' make up one of the major concerns of the Bible. The Old and New Testaments return again and again to topics like new directions, new beginnings and new life. And each of these topics is brought back to the central fact that it is the triune

God, the Father of Abraham and Isaac, the Logos, and the Spirit, who is the beginning of all things. The subject is so often raised because God was constantly leading his people into new places, both in their environment and in their spirit. So it was in history, and so it continues today.

All this means that this subject is an inexhaustible mine for Christian meditation, prayer and preaching. Therefore, there is no reason why a service on the theme of new beginnings should not have a regular place in the cycle of a congregation's year.

I approach the subject in different ways. Here is one approach which proved most helpful.

PASTORAL PRAYER

This was led by an Elder who himself had recently retired. Before he prayed he took one minute to reflect on three things:
- (1) The new experience of retirement;
- (2) The excitement it brought; for instance, some of the things he looked forward to doing in his retirement;
- (3) The nervousness he felt; for instance, a friend who retired shortly before him, had died before realising any of his retirement plans.

SERMON

At two points in the sermon, I was able to refer to things the children had said in our time together earlier in the service. Whether articulated or implied, the children and the comments they expressed were a living parable, adding reality to the address.

I noted that whenever I spoke of them, the children smiled broadly at me and those sitting near them. They almost certainly did not understand the sermon. What they did understand was that they had contributed to the worship experience and that their contribution was valued.

BENEDICTION

I asked the kinder people and the Elder who had led the prayer to come to the front of the church. I asked the children to once again stand on the form and hold hands. At one end of the line, I held a child's hand, and at the other end, the Elder also held a child's hand. This simple tableau proved to be a powerful visual culmination of the service. The congregation stood and we all sang together:–

1. This, this is the God we adore;
   our faithful, unchangeable friend;
   whose love is as great as his power,
   and neither knows measure nor end.
2. 'Tis Jesus the first and the last
   whose Spirit shall guide us safe home;
   we'll praise him for all that is past,
   and trust him for all that's to come.

Joseph Hart (1712-68)
The Australian Hymn Book, No. 153.

Chapter 3

Talking about terrible news

It had cost more lives than any other crash in aviation history. The planes involved were both jumbo jets and they crashed on an airport runway in the Canary Islands. More than five hundred people died and television crews were on hand to film the action. Soon the sight of burning bodies falling from the ruptured bellies of the giant planes was seen in countless millions of homes around the world. In my city, in the one week, television stations replayed the film three times on the early evening news. As far as they were concerned, the crash produced sensational film and it was to be used to saturation point. Perhaps the viewers most easily saturated were the young children. I guessed that most of the children in my suburb would have caught at least one run of the gruesome film.

On the following Sunday morning, when the children gathered around me at the front of the sanctuary, I took from the lectern the newspaper which carried the first pictures of the terrible crash. One picture filled the entire top half of the first page. There, in graphic detail, were the two giant planes locked together in a destructive embrace. I held up the picture for the children and then the congregation to view.

Turning to the children, I asked, 'Do any of you know about this?' Every child put up a hand. 'Would someone tell us about it?' A number of children were eager to talk about the event. Using the microphone, I allowed the children to talk about the crash. Each added a little extra detail. The tone of voice of some of the children clearly indicated they were still upset by the horror of the tragedy.

Returning to the lectern, I placed the photo where all the children and most of the adults could see it, then I asked, 'Do you think God made these aeroplanes crash?' In the pause which followed, I was aware that the church was suddenly 'pin drop' quiet. The children were puzzled by the question; some thought it was a trick. In all seriousness, I repeated the question. Their puzzlement continued.

A small girl put up her hand. 'No', she said. Others nodded in agreement. 'Why?' I asked. This time, a boy answered. 'God wouldn't do a thing like that.' It was my turn to agree.

'There is one big question, though, that many people would like to ask God', I said, 'and that is, if he loves us and wants to care for us like he says he does, why didn't he stop the planes from crashing?' Aware that this was a most difficult question, I nonetheless wanted to see if any child would venture an answer. Not one of them moved. After a pause, I said, 'That's a hard question!'

'Do you know, there are all kinds of bad things happening every day and someone is always asking, "If God loves us, why doesn't he stop it from happening?" I don't know what to say to that — except to say that the help I know God gives, is in the hearts and the minds of those who let him in. As far as I can see, most of the time, nearly all of the time, when things are going wrong, he doesn't interfere. Children, especially, need to be clear about that. Let me tell you why.'

I gave them an example. It had to do with prayers which they probably had heard their parents or their church pray for them. It concerned prayers in which adults ask God to watch over children and keep them safe. 'Because we pray for you like that, does that mean you can cross the road without looking? Will God place an invisible shield around the people who have been prayed for?' Some children laughed. In the interchange which followed, a number of children suggested ways in which God can help all of us to keep out of danger.

My concluding question to the children was, 'If there was a person you knew who was very sad today, because someone they loved died in this crash, is there anything you could do to help them?' The answers which followed touched on everything from cards to hugs. The message was clear through all of the responses of the children; they would be willing to do what they could to bring comfort.

Before the children returned to their seats, I asked them and all the congregation to sit quietly for a moment. I asked them to think of any person they knew who was sad at this time. I concluded this short time of silence with a brief prayer which went something like this:

Lord, we pray for all the sad people we know. We think of their names, and why they are sad. Help us to care about them as you care about them and to find ways of showing we care. Lord, we pray for all the people who are sad because of the accident we have been thinking about. We ask that each of them will have someone to love them and comfort them at this time.

We pray now for ourselves. Keep us safe from danger. Help us to keep watch and be always careful; and may we never cause danger for others.

We ask this in the name of Jesus, our friend and saviour. Amen.

THE SETTING

This topic was raised by the events of the preceding week. A monumental disaster, which had received extensive television coverage, left neither young nor old untouched by its horror or pathos. Primary school teachers had told me just how much it had been discussed at school. I felt it should be discussed in church.

To my mind, this needed to be done for the sake of the children, many of whom were frightened and worried by the event. Another reason for doing it was to show parents ways of talking with their children about the hard things of a sad world.

The timing of the segment was of crucial importance. Although I had something else planned for the Sunday in question, it had to be dropped. To talk about the crash two Sundays after the event would be to delay too long. The crash had to be raised while the shock was still present and the images vivid.

Hopefully, the story above will never be repeated. Nonetheless, every week, television and newspapers bring more bad news into our homes and parade it before our children. On some occasions, the graphic portrayal of appalling tragedies will cause particular worry to many children. When this happens, it is my belief that some discussion/meditation/prayer process should be used in church to help the children (and their parents) with the questions raised by the event. The approach I used in this chapter is only one way of doing this. Discussion on these matters need only be an occasional thing; in my case, I normally try not to raise a news story of this type more than once or twice a year.

When it comes to judging which story should be raised, I use the following criteria:

1. First and foremost, the news event must be known to the children before I raise it. The event will be one which I know has worried children and is currently the subject of anxious discussion amongst them.

2. In most cases, this will mean that scenes which are shocking and/or violent will have been re-run on news programs over a number of days.

In raising matters of this nature, it is not my purpose to draw the children's attention to the bad news in the world. Rather, I hope to help them cope with such matters as have been forced upon them by the news media in an immediate and frightening manner. For example, as I write, my mind goes to a recent Italian earthquake which devastated an entire region. Day after day, the early news ran extensive film on the devastation. Close-ups of persons in extreme grief and of corpses being removed from the rubble were seen by a million or more Australian children. Young children are very frightened by the idea that the earth could swallow their house, their parents or themselves. This anxiety must increase when, night after night, they see on their television sets this actually happening to real houses and real people. The result was that this particular disaster and the way it was presented on television created the kind of topic which many children would need to talk about.

There are some stories which meet the above criteria, and yet, are not suitable. A prime example is the Jonestown suicides. Another is that of the Yorkshire ripper. Undoubtedly, children know about these crimes, but personally I would not feel comfortable about briefly raising them in the context of a formal worship service.

3. Not all matters raised in this way need be about the loss of many lives. News coverage of devastating bushfires leaves a strong impression on minds young and old alike. I discussed this subject with the children one Sunday when bushfires were ravaging the state. On this occasion, two adults who had been in the thick of bad fires told of incidents of hardship and courage.

4. Although I have not yet attempted these myself, I believe that such enduring problems as inflation and unemployment are suitable subjects for discussion with children in church. I notice that

most children recognise each word and realise it is something to be concerned about.

In summary, before taking a news story to the children in church, I would want to be sure that it has already been a topic about which children have expressed concern at home or school. In actual fact, the news stories I have used in this way have found me; I did not have to find them. The story has been such that, over a number of days, it has shaken me, my house and the whole community.

RESOURCING THE WORSHIP

Due to the suddenness with which such stories are upon us, it is usually not possible to plan in advance a worship package which neatly integrates the news theme. Often, commitments will already have been made to worship themes, special segments or seasonal celebrations. In this situation, a news story will at first seem to sit awkwardly with other materials. In most cases, though, experience has shown that previously chosen scriptures and themes for that day can in a surprising way relate to, and help us understand, the issue which has been raised with the children.

Another factor which favours the weaving of the news subject into the worship is that the event will have also troubled the adults. As a general principle, all the concerns of life should be held up before God in worship. What is more, this should be done when a particular issue is 'hot' and not just on Remembrance Day or when mentioned in the collect of the day. Thus, the sharing of a news item of the week with the children should not be seen as an intrusion. It will rather be a legitimate contribution to the prayers and preaching of the day, whatever the church season or the readings in the lectionary.

When a news story of some shattering event is used in worship, the worship leaders must not think that they are expected to give instant, theological rhyme and reason for it. Our task is not to impart easy answers to life's most perplexing questions; rather, it is to help young and old in our congregations to enter into the pain and grief of those who suffer. Our weekly news of the world only reinforces what is so often quite plain in the Bible, that we live in a world in which misery and suffering is frequently heaped upon the innocent. It is important for our children to get the message that we must hold fast to our faith even when life seems to contradict it. Our adults also need to have this message reinforced again and again. The good news which remains constant is that in the face of inexplicable tragedy, it is the love of God which brings us together, holds us together, and in turn sends us out — not to be oracles, but to be messengers of healing.

In the service in which I talked with the children about the crash of the jumbos, I drew particular reference to it in two other ways:

A LITANY

This was one of intercession for those who suffered physical pain and the pain of grief. The responsive prayer I used made specific reference to people killed or injured in road accidents, and the victims of natural disasters.

PREACHING

As I had recently preached on the problem of suffering, I approached this subject from another perspective. I used the text from Psalm 90:12 — 'Teach us to count how few days we have and so gain wisdom of heart' (*Jerusalem Bible*). Also, this entire Psalm speaks powerfully of the frailty of human life and the necessity of receiving each day as a gift.

With the tragic crash as the background discussion, I developed three points:
    1. The unpredictable nature of life and our inability to foresee our length of days.
    2. The necessity of numbering (valuing) each day. This includes taking care lest we step into danger or bring danger to others.
    3. With God's help, we are to awake with joy each morning, filled with his love (Psalm 90:14), and willing to pass it on especially to those who suffer (Psalm 90:16).

In conclusion, I reminded everyone that the sermon was being preached in a world in which the crash of two jumbo jets was only one of the terrible things which had happened in the last week. Even so, as those in the congregation who had been through their own tragedy could testify, the love of God and of his people is the greatest healing force. His love is the hope in which we live and to which we are dedicated.

Chapter 4

Talking about surprises and presents

From my pocket, I produced a key on a piece of string. 'This has something to do with the most favourite thing I do every day. What do you think it is?' Comments from the children were 'driving in your car'; 'coming home after work'; 'going to the Post Office for the mail'. 'That's right', I said to the last comment. 'In fact, I have two keys for two post boxes. One is for me and one is for the place where I work.' How exciting it is to turn the key and see what mail has come today! One of the best feelings is not knowing just what will be inside the envelopes and packages in the post box. 'This came the other day.' I held up a brown business envelope. 'What sort of news could this envelope bring?' I asked the children, and invited two of them to come and join me to share their opinions. The ten-year-old boy spoke first. 'If it's bad news, it could be an electricity bill or a reminder to pay your telephone bill. If it's good news, it could be a letter from the Governor inviting you to his house or you've won a prize.' The second child was a pre-schooler. She stood on a chair so that she could share the same microphone as the boy. 'It could be a letter from your mother saying she is coming to visit you, or it could be just a letter from a friend.' Those very definite opinions were greeted by smiles from everyone. Everyone present could identify with at least the telephone account and news from a relative.

'Well, you're both very close to the truth. This envelope was good news for me, and in fact it is good news for all of us.' I read two or three sentences of a letter from a missionary who once was part of that congregation, then I asked the children, 'Have you ever received a nice surprise in the mail?' 'A birthday card with a clip-on brooch from an auntie I don't even know', responded the pre-schooler, and the ten-year-old eagerly described how he had won a prize in a breakfast cereal competition. 'Have you ever received bad or sad news?' No, but Mum or Dad or friends had. I thanked the children for their contribution, and reached to lift into view two very important props.

'Today is about surprises, and there is a surprise in each of these gift boxes.' One was large and properly gift-wrapped; that is, the paper was coloured and there was a large bow on top. The other was small in every dimension, wrapped in brown paper, and unmarked.

'Would someone like to unwrap the gift box of their choice?' Of course, all of the children wanted to help out with this task. As I beckoned to one of them, I added, 'One of these contains something that all of you can share. Just wait and see which one is chosen'. My guess is that most people present would have thought for a little while that the best choice was in the plain wrapping, but who could resist the bright wrapping and the biggest box? My young friend couldn't, and proceeded to unwrap it. I had placed the gifts at a level all could see. She lifted from the box an average-sized grapefruit. 'Not the greatest of presents' was the message on her face, and from the faces of all the children, that opinion was unanimous. 'Who would like to unwrap the small one?' This had to be the best present. Yes, inside was a Swiss chocolate block with enough squares for all the children to have a piece after church. I added that there might be enough for adults too, if the children were enterprising in their breaking up of the squares. 'Would you ask your Sunday school teacher to help you do this?' I asked my helper as she left the microphone. With a smile, I held up the grapefruit. 'Sometimes, what is on the inside isn't quite what we expect by a look at the outside.'

THE WORST TASTING ORANGES IN THE WORLD

'I'd like to tell you about the very worst tasting oranges. When I was small, I was a member of the local Brownie Pack. That's like a junior Girl Guides group. Every Saturday afternoon, there was a Brownie meeting, and we did all sorts of interesting things. The part I liked best about Brownies was our meeting place. It was a little hut in a green field. The field had many different bushes and trees, and it was on one of these trees that I discovered the worst tasting oranges. The orange tree was in the corner of the field. When I noticed it, it must have been the season for oranges. They seemed to cover the branches, yellow in colour rather than orange, and very, very big. I used to wonder why no-one picked them, or at least why no-one seemed interested in having one to eat. Perhaps the orange tree didn't belong to the Brownie Club, and, if someone else owned the tree, they certainly didn't like oranges.

'Well, one afternoon, I decided that some of those oranges would make a very nice present for my mother. "Do the Brownies own this land?" I asked. Oh yes, we certainly did! Good, I thought, but I didn't feel quite confident enough to follow my question with "Then, can I take some of those oranges on that tree in the far corner home to my mother?" My friend and I waited till all the other Brownies had gone. My friend picked and I packed until I filled my Brownie bag. It looked just like this (I held up a cloth Brownie bag which belonged to one of the children in Brownies). The oranges were so big that six filled the bag. I picked a seventh to eat on the way home. It was a very warm day and I imagined just how sweet and refreshing the orange juice would be for the long walk home. Under a shady tree about half way home, we stopped for the treat. It was quite exciting peeling off the skin. They really were the biggest and most yellow oranges I had ever seen. Then my first taste. Oh! It was so terrible and so sour! I could hardly believe that what looked so good, could taste so bad. I didn't arrive home very excited. "Here's a surprise, Mum, that was supposed to be a good one, but it's not." She opened my Brownie bag and looked as pleased as I was at first. "They're not what you think — they taste awful — the worst oranges ever."

'Well, that day I learned about grapefruit.' I held up the grapefruit that had been in the gift box. 'Mum happened to like grapefruit. Yes she did, and I enjoyed the pie she made from them the next day.

'I wonder if any of you have become excited about a television or radio advertisement for a toy; perhaps for the adults, it's a new brand of detergent or a new car. It sounded like a good thing to buy and a terrific bargain, but when you saw it or used it, it wasn't as good as the advertisement said.'

Two different children shared their stories briefly. I thanked them and concluded: 'There are lots of things in life that come in ways we least expect. Sometimes we are disappointed at first appearances, but when we take a deeper look inside, we discover many good things. Sometimes, the best presents will come in ways we least expect. In every day, there are wonderful things and wonderful people in what seem ordinary places.'

Jesus really cared about what was on the inside. I recalled Matthew 5: 5-9, read a few minutes prior to the time with the children. That's the best present we can give to each other and to God. God's best surprise gift of all was Jesus and he came to the world in a very plain wrapping. No one expected God's son to be born in a stable.

We closed with a prayer. This was printed on an *Order of Service* sheet. Everyone read together:

> Thank you for the good surprises in our lives.
> Help us when we receive bad news, or are disappointed by things.
> Help us to look more on the inside than on outward appearance.
> Help us to care about people's thoughts and feelings.
> Today, we remember the way Jesus came into the world.
> Today, we invite him to come inside our hearts and our thoughts.
> This we pray as your family. Amen.

THE SETTING

One of the most delightful Christmas gifts I received last Christmas was a wall-hanging. It consisted of the front of a used Christmas card, silver paper, the cardboard backing of an old notebook, cotton braid, wool and glue. Yes, it was a gift from a child. The most valued birthday present this year was a home-made wallet. There are more pockets than you would believe, and a gold Letraset 'P' imprinted on the front right corner. It is a present from an adult with the spirit of a child.

The giving and receiving of surprises and presents is an experience available to everyone. For adults, it holds as much enchantment as for children. And there isn't a child who doesn't love to give presents as well as receive them. They are masters at plotting surprises; they always want to bring happiness and to make peace.

Although I first introduced this subject in church a month after Christmas, it was the Christmas season with all its present exchanging that stirred my thoughts in this direction.

These were my contemplations as I prepared 'Talking about Surprises and Presents':

    a. Television, for many children, is the shop-window of life's playground. So much is advertised as the 'best quality', 'best bargain ever', 'absolutely essential for the joys of life', be it toys, diet, clothes, or food.

The message is, 'Get this and be more popular, trendy and happy'. It is not true, but the beautiful selling pitch would convince any child otherwise. I hoped to draw on the Christmas season's intensified advertising of this kind, to alert in children the powers of discernment and choice.

    b. The message that 'the biggest and most expensive gift is the best gift', although wrong, is very dominant and children believe it.

I wished to encourage and affirm those who liked to make things, who spent time contriving beautiful surprises from seemingly plain and useless objects, and who prepared these as a fine gift. This, I hoped, would also encourage adults to see the wonderful value of gifts made by their children. The scribble on the crumpled piece of paper is, to the child, a work of art for the one they love.

    c. Every parent wants his or her child to have the very best that life can afford.

What this means, for many parents, is bigger and more expensive birthday and Christmas presents, better life insurance policies, the best schools and the best training in social graces.

I hoped to speak indirectly to the adults in the congregation about some other wonderful gifts to give their children; the gift of being able to create fun and fellowship with their own resources; the gift of deriving meaning and pleasure from what seems like plain and very ordinary surroundings; the gift of sharing with their children the beliefs, places and people that have central importance in their own lives.

As someone who is committed to the mass media and its presence in our lives, in no way did I want my message to come across as a scourging of television and radio for children. Despite my efforts, there were one or two parents who, as a result of the service, wanted to sell their T.V. sets the next day. You can imagine how popular I was with their children! Nevertheless, I feel that the subject is important enough to persevere with, and to introduce at least once a year to a congregation.

RESOURCING THE WORSHIP

One of the things I am most passionate about in my work with congregations is spelling out the concept of the church being seen and experienced as 'A People to Belong to' or an extended family. When a congregation sees itself as a people and lives out its life and witness in this way, to me that's about the finest gift we give our children.

However, in this service, I did not want the children to feel that I was talking to the adults about them. That would be a very clear signal that, apart from my time with the children, the rest of the worship hour was of the 'adults only' variety. Also, I was enthusiastic about enabling the children to see that within Jesus' family, there were wonderful surprises and gifts, some lasting a lifetime. Thus, in the sermon, I drew particular reference to the visual aids I had used earlier with the children.

PREACHING

'It would be very sad if our church were like this', and I held high the gift wrapped box to develop these comparisons:

1. The outside is big and very beautiful and well kept;
2. The messages on the noticeboard are inviting;
3. You would expect to find something or someone very wonderful inside (at this point, I opened the box and once again showed the grapefruit);
4. But when folk come, alone or with their children, they find it very different from the outside appearance and the messages on the noticeboard don't seem to apply. They do not recognise the gifts we have to offer them and sometimes we do not know them ourselves.

'It would also be very sad if our Church was like this', and this time, I showed the small box with the plain wrapping and made comparisons. If our gift to this community is so camouflaged that it blends with the rest of the community unnoticed or unattractive; where else can folk go to find Jesus and his family, a people to belong to?

Although the Epistle reading, 1 Peter 2 (*R.S.V.*), was the broad basis of the sermon, I chose as the Gospel, Matthew 23:27-28:

'How terrible for you, teachers of the Law and Pharisees! You hypocrites! You are like whitewashed tombs, which look fine on the outside but are full of bones and decaying corpses on the inside. In the same way, on the outside you appear good to everybody, but inside you are full of hypocrisy and sins.'

This enabled me to recall the gift boxes and was helpful to adults; it was also readily appreciated by the children who responded attentively to the illustration. As I concluded, I placed the two boxes side by side, and reflected: regardless of whether our church is ornate and grand, or spartan and small in its appearance, when we gather together for worship, it is who we are and how we celebrate that is really important.

By the grace of God, we are his people among whom the gift of wholeness and family can be offered to everyone. If you like, it's the most needed gift and often the least expected.

A RETURN-OFFERING ENVELOPE

Everyone in the congregation received a sheet of paper about the size of an aerogram. The idea was that people could write on one side and then fold it up into an envelope. On the 'outside', they would write 'To ... with love from ...'. The sheets of paper were distributed with pencils as the offering was taken up.

As part of the offering announcement, I explained that each person was to receive an envelope and pencil. When everyone had both in their possession, I led them through the task.

'Can you turn this envelope into a surprise gift for someone who would least expect it from you, but someone who is part of this congregation? It may be that this is more difficult than buying a gift in a shop. This gift must be something you can express in writing — a prayer, a promise, a comforting word. It could be saying, you're sorry. Perhaps you don't even know the name of this person, only their face is familiar to you — call that person 'a friend'. I ask all of you (any time before you go home) to pass that envelope to the one for whom it is intended. In the silence, let's all write. Those who are very small may like to draw what they would like to say.'

I followed the silence with a prayer of dedication of our gifts and of our lives.

WHAT I'D LIKE TO GIVE TO MY CHURCH

This was the title of a very simple audio-visual presentation — perhaps no more than 90 seconds long — that preceded the prayers of confession and intercession. It was prepared by the Sunday school in three stages.

1. About fifteen children contributed a one-sentence statement on 'what I'd like to give my church'. These sentences were recorded using an exterior microphone plugged into a portable cassette player (use of a pause button after each child had spoken eliminated the space between comments).

2. The children then expressed 'what I'd like to give my church' in picture form on small pieces of acetate cut from shirt boxes and mounted in slide frames, using fine point, overhead projector pens.

3. The statements and slides were matched, in sequence, ready for the service.

As the cassette played through the public address system and the slides passed through on the screen, I was aware of two levels of response. The children felt complimented and glowed with pride at their contribution. From the adults came smiles and ripples of laughter for some of the comments. For others, there was silence; the commitment and spirit of the children moved them deeply.

. . . I would give to my church a book of songs.
. . . I would give a new Communion table to my church.
. . . I would give my voice to the church choir.
. . . I would bring flowers to the church.
. . . I would give money.
. . . I would give a new wine bottle.
. . . I would give a promise.
. . . I would say a prayer for my church.
. . . I would give love.
. . . I would give myself.
. . . I would give my gift to Jesus.

Chapter 5

Talking about precious things

The numbers in the congregation were not any more than last Sunday; there just seemed to be more bodies.

The previous Sunday, I had invited all the small children to bring their favourite cuddly toy to church next Sunday. Well, that great day had arrived. The congregation was positively abeam with the smiling faces of children. There were other heads abob as well. Peering from the crook of every small and loving arm was the head of any one of an enormous variety of soft toys.

I had issued two stipulations along with the last Sunday's invitation: one, the cuddly toy was to be a silent one; two, this was not to be a regular event, but a one Sunday special! My intention at the time was not only to give the children a framework for their expectations, but also to appease any adults whose hackles may have raised at the prospect of worship in a toy shop for several Sundays. As I gazed over the congregation, my fears were allayed. Certainly, there were nervous postures, but sheer pleasure and interest were the dominant expressions.

The reading of the first lesson was generally the signature tune for 'Talking About Something Important'. Because it wasn't always appropriate or necessary for the children to come to the front, they waited for the invitation.

On this particular morning, they strained on the edge of the pews. Some of the more enterprising children had taken the very front seats before the worship had even begun.

'The subject of my time with the children this morning is not a surprise to any of you. Thank you, children, for bringing your favourite cuddly toy. Before you come and join me here at the front, I have something important to ask of you. All of us here like teddies, and toys that are soft like teddies. Could you show your cuddly toy to an adult who is here this morning — not your parents — someone who hasn't seen it before? Tell them its name, and how long it's been with you. They may even like to hold it. As there are not enough teddies for every adult, show yours to two or three who are sitting together. Move quietly and talk in whispers. If you would prefer not to show anyone, that's fine.'

Only two remained, holding tightly to a teddy and sitting quietly. As I moved down to chat with them, I was joined by one of the adults. Two minutes passed. From the front of the church, I began to sing (actually half sing and half speak);

'I've got to get in touch with the way I feel,
Get in touch with the way that I feel.
Got to get in touch with the way that I feel,
Get in touch with the way that I feel,
Get in touch with the way that I feel.
May I get in touch with the way that you feel?
May I read your feelings today?
If we can both get in touch with the way that we feel,
We will grow close together in love.
We will grow close together in love.'

Carey Landrey, *'Hi, God!'*

As I sang, conversation faded then ceased altogether. The organist who had rehearsed the flow of events with me prior to the service, haltingly followed the tune as agreed.

'Children, would you like to come and join me?' As they eagerly approached the front of the church, I noticed that some of the eleven year olds who had done the adult thing and left their cuddly toys in the corner of the bedroom, were among their number.

My first question was addressed to the adults. 'Is there someone who is willing to share their conversation?' Yes, there were a few. I chose the oldest of the volunteers to join me. Turning to the children, I asked, 'Who talked to the lady and showed her their soft toy?' A small boy leapt to his feet and so did his large, somewhat soiled, Panda-toned bear. Briefly, these two new friends told the congregation the teddy's name, their names, the teddy's age and the favourite things it liked to do. Last of all, the old lady said, 'When I was small, I had a golliwog that I loved until it fell to pieces'.

I thanked both of them and walked to the lectern where I produced a large paper bag. 'I have brought three things to show you.' I held high a platypus, a dog and a small, standard teddy bear.

'This platypus belongs to my nine year old neighbour. He loves cuddly toys and a few days ago, we talked about that. This is what he said.' At that moment, I pressed the play-button of the cassette P.A. system. (In places where there isn't that facility, or where there is no recorded interview, a verbal recalling of a conversation is equally effective.)

'Bradley, what makes you like the soft toys?'

'When you're itchy, you just put them against you and rub and they do some good.'

'Do you do anything else with your soft toys?'

'Yes, have parties with them, make some sprinkle sandwiches and they eat the sprinkle sandwiches because one's got a hole in his mouth and the food comes through to my hand when I have my hand there.'

'Do you take soft toys to bed with you?'

'Yes.'

'Some people think that boys shouldn't have soft animals. What do you think about that?'

'I think they're wrong, 'cause I keep all my toys good and use them from when I was a little boy and every child has a teddy when he's a little boy and likes it, and I still like mine.'

'If you're sad, does your teddy help you at all?'

'Yes, 'cause if I don't want to play with my sister or any of my friends, I play with them.'

'Can adults be in your pretend land with all your toys as well?'

'Yes, if anyone says that people can't love teddies when they're old, my Mum's still got her teddy.'

'Why do you think adults hang on to things like that?'

'So they can give them to their children and show them.'

'Do you feel good when Mum does that for you?'

'Yes, at Christmas a few years ago when I was about three, she showed her teddy to me.'

'When a teddy gets ugly, do you still love it?'

'Yes.'

'How come that is?'

'Cause they still comfort you and all that when you're sad.'

When the interview finished, I allowed two of the children to respond with their comments about cuddles that comforted when they were sad, and the cuddly toys that a parent had kept for many years to give to them.

It was time to talk about the second of my soft toy requisitions.

'This one is mine', and I held high the floppy eared dog. 'This was a gift from a child. Do you know, it's the first soft toy I've ever owned. Oh, I had lots of dolls, but not anything like this.'

'When she gave it to me, I went to place it on the centre of my bed but my young friend said, "No, you must cuddle it first". She took it from me and held it very close. "Just like this." (I demonstrated to everyone) and then she added, "Pauline, you cuddle this dog just like you cuddle a person." That was a very nice thing to say, I thought.' Heads in the congregation and among the children before me were nodding in agreement.

I held up the last of the three soft toys. 'This little teddy is seven years old and so is the owner. Darryl is the owner's name and the teddy is called Terial. Now, that's a most unusual name. I'll tell you why it came to be that.

'When this teddy was about two years old, its fur began to wear out. There was no possibility that this teddy could be replaced by a new one with soft fur. Oh no, it was too special — just like a member of the family. So Darryl's Mum re-covered this little fellow with material. Darryl thought this sounded like a great name for his teddy, but he could only say the second part of the word: 'Terial'. Do you know Terial has been covered three more times since then, and still he's the one Darryl loves the best. Can you guess why that is?'

The responses from the children were those of tried and tested experience:

'It doesn't matter what your teddy looks like, you love it all the more when it's been with you a long time.'

'A teddy is like a very good friend — you don't run out on them.'

As I propped up all three soft toys — platypus, dog and little teddy — on the edge of the lectern, I asked another question. 'Is that the way people are with each other?'

Bending down with my microphone, three children offered their opinions. The buoyant atmosphere had subsided. A deep thoughtfulness had rested upon the children;

'No, not always, some people don't like the way you look, or they get sick of you so they won't be your friend.'

'Sometimes, when you're crying and you're very sad, it's hard to talk to someone. They mightn't understand.'

'But a teddy will?' I queried.

'Not really, but when there's no one there, a teddy's good to have. It's like they're listening.'

'My best friend and I — we can't stop being with each other — that's as good as a teddy. When a person is not very kind and won't be your friend, you need a teddy to cuddle.'

Quietly I responded: 'Yes, you're right. People aren't always the friends they ought to be. That includes all of us here today. Even at church, we sometimes forget about the feelings of others, or are so impatient with the way other people think or act that we don't even try to be a friend. But wouldn't it be sad if all we had to cuddle was a teddy?' The children nodded enthusiastically.

'For some of us, it's very hard to show our love. Even shaking a hand firmly, putting an arm around someone or letting them comfort us can be very difficult. The hardest thing of all is to say "I love you". Yet that's just about the most important and most wonderful thing to say.'

I picked up the floppy eared dog. 'The little friend who gave me this was right.' I hugged the dog tightly to me. 'This is the way people need us to be to them in our hearts. It doesn't mean we go around hugging everyone, but rather we care and feel love for them.'

Then I held Terial high above my head. 'There is someone who never gets tired of us; and whose love for us never wears out. He knows our name; he knows our thoughts; he loves us when we're glad; he loves us when we're sad; he loves us when we're bad. That someone is Jesus.

'Terial has had four new coverings. Jesus makes people whole and new again. That's what becoming a Christian means.

'He fills us with love. That love is for others and that love helps us to be gentle and kind. Through the way we are, others will come to know about God's love. Here in God's family, it is Jesus' love and forgiveness that keeps us together and makes us strong.

'Children, thank you for bringing your cuddly toys and sharing your love for them with us. Always, we want you to feel that here, we are your friends and that Jesus is your friend.

'I often sing a little song. It helps me remember all these things. It's like a prayer. I want it to be your prayer today. I will say the words, then sing them.' I looked up at the congregation. 'Could you sing with me?'

> Into my heart,
> into my heart,
> come into my heart, Lord Jesus,
> come in today, come in to stay,
> come into my heart, Lord Jesus.

THE SETTING

I was very nervous about bringing the subject of teddy bears and soft toys into worship. People have even expressed caution at reading the title of the chapter. To my mind, it was still an important subject for both children and adults, and its potential for contributing to the meaning of the whole worship was sufficient for it to be the focus of my time with the children; but the possibility of it appearing frivolous and childish was not remote either. The topic would require some sensitive preparation. However, as you can see, I took the risk.

These were the reasons why I saw the risk as worthwhile.

1. Teddies are universally important to children. Without exception, on the first or second visit to a child's home, out come the soft toys. It may be only one, the favourite, or it may be a great array of sizes, colours and shapes. Always they are an instant source of conversation and play a very natural friendship-building role.

2. Teddies are often an important part of the private world of children's dreams and affections. They are there when the child

goes to sleep at night; there when the child wakes with a nightmare. To all the children I have talked to, teddies are good friends when they are sad, and when they play in their private fantasy world behind a closed door. Talking with them about their soft toys, I believed, would be speaking to thoughts and feelings that were very close to their hearts.

3. As more children talked with me and showed me their soft toys in their homes, I realised that many of their parents had kept a soft toy from their own childhood. Teenagers too, though not inclined to cuddle soft toys, were not shy about using them to decorate the bedroom. Therefore, to take teddies into worship would in no way cut off the older members of the congregation. I was convinced that somewhere a soft toy or similar object had figured in their childhood play and affections.

4. The intimacy and fidelity that mark the relationship between a child and its teddies is a revelation of the tenderness and love that fills the child's spirit. I hoped this would be evident to all at worship, and that its effect would be two fold:

— a reminder to the adults of the childrens warmth and tenderness would recall to the adults similar feelings and experiences of their own childhood years;

— enabling the children to share their cuddly toys and inviting the adults to hold them, would provide an opportunity for adults to feel comfortable, and show to the children their own expressions of affection and love.

One particular event in my home confirmed this. I recalled some of this with the children earlier in this chapter. A child had presented me with a soft floppy-eared dog, very attractive and nice to feel. However, when she asked me to cuddle it, I realised it had been a long time since I had done something like that. It must have been very obvious to her that I felt very uncomfortable and rather foolish in my half-hearted hugging attempts. She softly rebuked me for not doing the proper and natural thing with the dog, which, of course, was to hold and hug it tightly. Then, she demonstrated exactly how it should be done, coupling this with wisdom from the mouths of babes: 'You cuddle the dog just like you cuddle a person!'

Without a doubt, sensitive use of this subject could build stronger bonds of family love across the generations.

The following familiar experience gave another dimension to this subject. I once visited my young brother, Daniel, who at the time was eight years of age. I watched him make his bed and then proceed to decorate the bed covers with a small colony of soft toys.

'Where did you get this one?' I asked, holding up a Koala bear.

'Oh, that's Joanne's.' (Joanne is his sister.)

'And what about this one?'

'That's Joanne's too.'

Each time I asked about the cuddly toys, Danny's accent became more gruff telling me about the ownership of these toys. Either one sister or the other owned them.

'I didn't realise just what this conversation meant until he added, 'I want a cuddly toy, but everyone says that there's lots of other things I can do besides play with teddy bears'. 'Oh!' I said, 'I think it's very good for boys to play with cuddly toys, just as good as it is for girls or for men and women'. I then added, 'I like cuddly toys, Danny, and in fact, I've only just got one from a little girl'. He seemed most interested.

Later in the day, I overheard him in conversation with his mother. 'Mum, could you get me a cuddly toy of my own? Pauline says it's alright for boys my age; in fact, she said any age could have one of their very own.' It wasn't one of those quiet conversations either! Danny was close to tears.

My next visit to Danny was some months later. When I arrived, he rushed to greet me, with a lion in his arms, a soft cuddly lion.

Danny plays soccer, gets in the occasional brawl at school. But his heart is soft and tender, and like every child, he wants to give love and receive it even in his play. There are many Australian men, many in our churches, who have grown up believing that it is effeminate to express love or to show their feelings, and there are many parents who discourage their boys from cuddling any toy, beyond the age of five. Another message of reassurance that I wished to incorporate as I talked with the children was that no one is ever too old or too masculine to be warm, affectionate and loving.

As children play, they are preparing for life. I was taking their play and their lives very seriously as I invited them to bring their teddies and cuddly toys to church that Sunday morning.

RESOURCING THE WORSHIP

It was never my intention to extend the visual imagery of teddy bears or their soft cuddly relatives into the rest of the worship hour. With my limited confidence in the response I expected from the congregation, I was sure that many would breathe a sigh of relief when this 'Teddy Bears Picnic' concluded. Thus, indirect reference was the approach I chose to follow and on reflection this proved to be a powerful recipe.

'Which ways of touching are of the spirit of Jesus?' was the underlying theme threading the segments of the worship together.

BIBLE READINGS

The lessons of the day focused on Christ's compassion, humility and greatness: Ephesians 3; Philippians 3. The story of the woman with a haemorrhage who was healed when she touched Jesus was read prior to my time with the children (Luke 8:42-48).

MEDITATION ON HANDS

For prayers of confession and intercession, I led a meditation on hands. I invited the congregation to feel their own hands, and led them through a time of reflection.

'Some of you have more lines to feel than others; perhaps the skin you can feel is like leather; hands that have weathered many years and much work. These are the hands of the old. Some have hands that are soft and tender; these are the hands of the very young.

'Feel for the callouses and think about the work that caused these callouses, and offer this to God. Feel for the cracks and scars; think about the hurt and brokenness of your life. Confess your sins and ask for healing.

'Feel the lines of your palm and think of your life's journey. Remember those in our community who are never touched in a loving way.
'Some hands here are slender, some stout, some calloused, some smooth; they are your hands and they are beautiful. They are the hands of Jesus. May we reach out in love and may our touch be that of tenderness and compassion. May we be God's instruments of healing and hope. God help us, we pray. In Jesus' name. Amen.'

SERMON

The title seemed to be at the other extreme to a 'Talking About Precious Things'. It was 'External Ceremonies or Faith Within?' I was aware of two extreme attitudes evident in many Christians to which I wanted to speak, and which I wanted to challenge. The first was that Christian love can be reduced to the denominator of sentimentality; the second was that Christianity can be carried 'in the head', i.e. knowing the Bible verses and intellectualising the principles of faith is sufficient.

Certainly there was much that children could not understand. But woven into the twenty minutes were illustrations that brought a response of raised heads and bright eyes from even the young children. They were drawn from these points:

The strength of Jesus' person and the wisdom of his speech was matched by the compassion and tenderness in his heart and in his actions. (I related elements of the story involving Danny).

Our faith is not an intellectual acceptance; it fills our heart and spills out in our love and compassion for others.

Towards the end of the sermon, I held up an old teddy, the one-leg, one-eye variety. (I had asked a member of the congregation who had kept such a teddy from childhood if I could use it as part of the sermon of the day. I especially looked for one in disrepair.)

With this visual focus, I recounted the restoring love of Jesus; the love that sees within; Jesus' love for the unlovely; the challenge to reach out and welcome to our embrace the broken and unloved.

A LITANY

At the close of the sermon, I invited the congregation to respond in a special way to the Apostles' creed. I would read one or two lines and the congregation's response would be, 'Lord, this I believe. This is my creed.'

Everyone stood. I began, 'I believe in God, the Father almighty, creator of heaven and earth'. The congregation readily responded, 'Lord, I believe. This is my creed.'

It seemed that folk were a little reluctant to move from the church that morning. Why? Along the pews were many small huddles of adults and children. In the middle of each were one or two small cuddly toys, no doubt the topic of every conversation; and not to forget the cuddly toys that were not there. Those that were owned and loved by the adults in their childhood. They were certainly getting a mention!

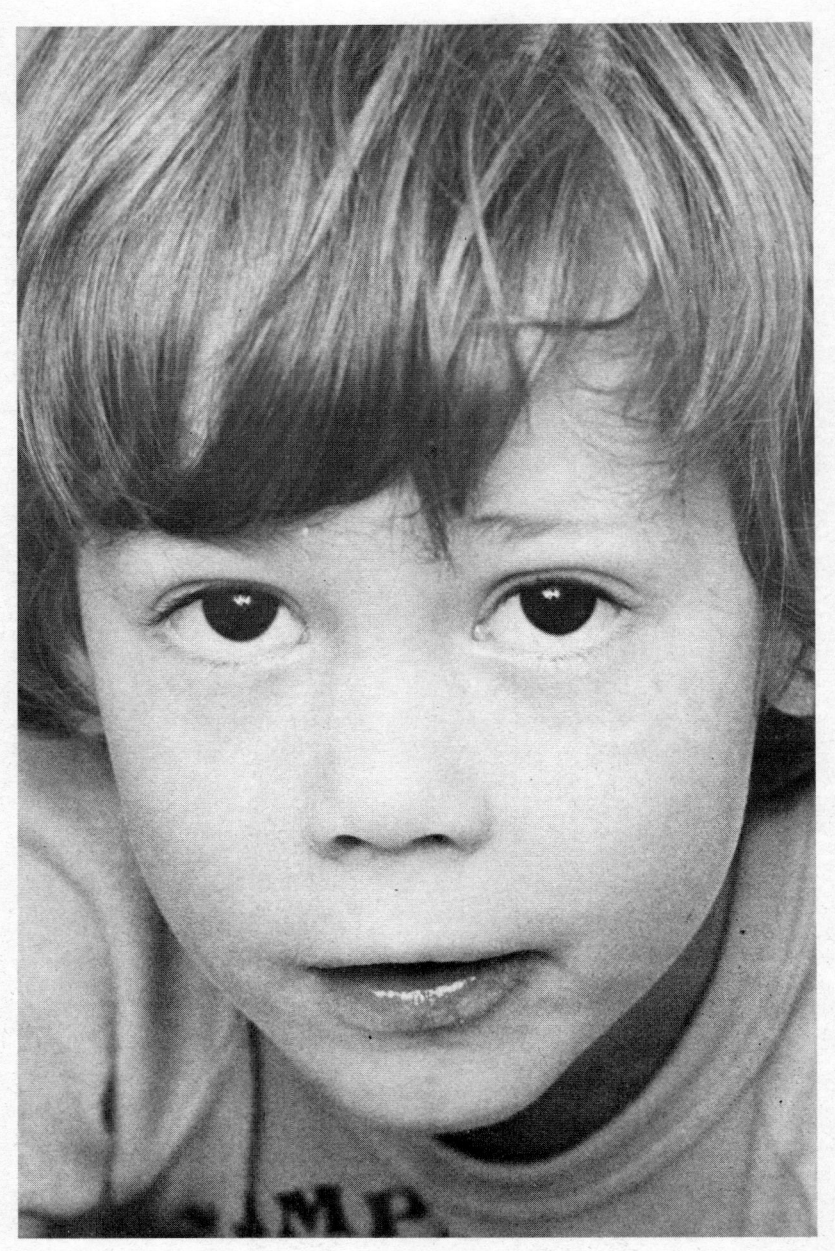

Chapter 6

Talking about the death of someone important

These children were not used to coming to the front to be with the minister, and had come forward only with reluctance. Besides, I was new to them and we had not yet become friends. 'Do any of you have pictures of people in your bedrooms?' I asked. No one moved. Some looked at me with unblinking stares; others looked down. 'What about a poster of a singer or a pop group?' Now I knew an answer was near. A little five year old called out, 'Abba'. 'How many of you have a picture of Abba in your bedrooms?' I enquired. My memory is that every hand went up.

'What do you like about Abba?' I asked. The group of children came to life. They all had an answer. 'Good singers', 'They sing happy songs', 'They look pretty', 'They dance'. Lacking a microphone, I had to repeat their answers out loud to enable the congregation to hear. 'How many of you would like to be like Abba when you grow up?' Three girls immediately put up their hands. One boy sneaked his hand half-way up. I took from the lectern a paper tube with a rubber band around it. Taking off the band, I unrolled a poster. I took care to keep the picture towards me and away from the children. I announced, 'This is a picture of a pop singer who is important to me. Would any of you like to guess who?' 'Abba', called out the little girl who had spoken up first. Other guesses followed, but none was correct. I turned the poster toward them, and they saw the black-haired young man with the gorgeous blue suit. As if with one voice, two children called out, 'Elvis'.

'Do any of you know some news about Elvis?' I asked. I chose the hand of a child who had not yet spoken. 'He died this week', he said. 'How many of you knew that?' I asked. All but the smallest children knew about poor Elvis. 'You may be wondering why I have his picture with me this morning.' Frowning faces in the congregation told me that some adults were pondering that very question. Their looks seemed to be telling me, 'What is a picture of a man like that doing in a place like this?'

Fixing the poster on the back of the lectern, I began to tell the children and the congregation about Elvis and me. I told how Elvis was the first pop star I ever had thought anything about. I recounted my memory of a conversation which took place in my teen years. Some young workmates were shocked when I confessed that I had never heard of 'Elvis the Pelvis'. From that day forward, it seemed to me that his voice was on every radio station, and his picture was in every magazine.

'Elvis and I grew up together; by that, I mean at the same time', I told them. 'The big difference was that he was rich and famous by the time he was twenty, and I was just another young man who had not made a success at anything.' I told them how many records he had sold, how much money he had made and how many cars he owned. The children were impressed. 'I would have given anything to swap places with Elvis. Do you think your parents would have ever liked to change places with Elvis?' I asked. No answer was forthcoming. 'Why don't you ask them after church?'

I explained that for many people of my age, Elvis used to be for them, what Abba was for today's children and teenagers. The children were looking hard at me. They were checking my face just in case I was tricking them. 'It's true', I said, 'and if Elvis wasn't your parents' favourite, they probably had another pop star who used to be as important to them as Abba is to you'.

'Now I am glad I didn't get my wish to change places with Elvis. Can any of you guess why?' One boy knew: 'Because now you would be dead'. I went on to ask the children did they think Elvis would have ever liked to change places with an ordinary person like me, or their parents. They found that idea hard to believe. I told them that when a person becomes rich and famous, they often find that fame brings with it lots of problems. As an example, I told them of the security system that surrounded Elvis night and day.

'Did you know that lots of people sometimes wish they were different or that they came from a different family?' I asked. The children looked surprised. 'I suppose that everybody does that once in a while. When I was small, I used to wish I was not in a family which went to church. I used to think of how good it must be to play all day Sunday. Christians seemed to miss out on so many things. Do you ever feel like that?' I asked. I couldn't tell what the children in front of me were thinking. Out of the corner of my eye, I saw a couple of junior teens nodding in vigorous agreement. 'That might be the kind of feeling you get when you think you would like to grow up and be like Abba. That was the kind of feeling I got as a young person when I felt I would like to swap places with Elvis.'

I began to roll up the poster. As I did so, I talked about the sadness I felt when Elvis died. 'It's not that I still want to swap places with him', I said. 'I had given up that idea a long time ago. When he died, it was as though a kind of hero from my youth had died.'

'Would you like to hear me sing the first song I ever heard Elvis sing?' No child expressed an opinion, but I could see some adults wagging their heads. Undeterred, I sang:

If you're feeling lonely,
and you've got no place to dwell,
just take a walk down lonely street,
to Heartbreak Hotel;
I get so lonely I could die.

'Did you know that a person can die of loneliness? Some people think that is what killed Elvis', I said. I talked about Jesus' claim that he came to give people 'abundant' life; a life that was full up with good things. I told how, as a child, I used to find this hard to believe. For instance, whatever could Jesus give me that would be anywhere near as good as being a film star or a pop singer? 'Well', I said, 'I know one thing that Jesus gives that you can't be sure of having if you become a famous entertainer, and that is a family with friends of all ages to care for you. Perhaps if Elvis had found a family like that, he would be still alive today.'

Once again, I unrolled the poster and fixed it on the lectern, only this time the white back of the poster faced the congregation. I asked the children and adults to help me make a list of people who were very lonely. Starting first with our community, we then thought about our country, and finally, lonely people in other countries. Adults added their suggestions to those given by the children. About eight different situations of loneliness were mentioned. I told the congregation that these suggestions would be used later in the service. I left the list of lonely people attached to the lectern for the remainder of the service.

My concluding comments dwelt on the fact that life for famous singers is often not as much fun as it looks on television or the posters. 'Everyone now knows that for Elvis, life was not all fun', I said, 'and it's probably not all fun for Abba either. The life Jesus gives us with his family may not look as exciting as the shiny life of the beautiful people on the posters', I said, 'but the good thing is that it gets better and brighter the longer we live it'.

THE SETTING

The death of Elvis shook all my generation, including me. It's not as though I was a great fan of his, but it was, I think, because for us, he was one of the symbols of our generation. I am not sure whether the age in which we lived shaped Elvis, or whether Elvis shaped the age. Certainly, there was a joint inter-action between the two. It seemed to me that for my contemporaries, Elvis lived out or embodied the definition of what it was like to have a good time. Whatever you thought of his music, there was no denying that it had brought him all the material goods and pleasures of this world. The truck driver who had sung and wriggled his way to the top was someone to be noted. I suspect that for millions, either consciously or subconsciously, he was living proof that it is possible to live for fun, fun, fun. For those who believed this, the death of Elvis must have been a shattering blow. Even people who were not impressed by 'fun', Elvis style, were not immune to his influence. Like him or hate him, few persons could have grown up in the 50s and 60s, and been unaware of him and what he represented. For one reason or another, most of his generation found reason for thought in his death.

To older children, Elvis had been little more than a shadowy figure in the pop world. Many younger children would have never heard of him. The media coverage of his death changed this. His name was suddenly on everyone's lips — including the children's. Not that his death touched them; they were simply interested in this news from the pop world. If the news affected anyone in their house, most likely it would have been their parents.

At the time of Elvis' death, Abba mania was sweeping Australia. Whatever parents thought about them, it seemed there was nothing they could do to resist the influence of this group on their children. Let parents and teachers beware, children would allow no word to be spoken against this golden group. Abba's larger-than-life lurex image had dazzled its way into the children's brains and nothing could eclipse them.

I know that quite a number of parents were at that time having running arguments with their children about Abba. The death of Elvis brought to my mind similar arguments between parents and children and young people about him. Certainly in his early days, Elvis was a figure of which nice parents greatly disapproved. I can remember stories of family rows which centred on buying Elvis records or attending Elvis movies.

It was this all-pervasive influence of Abba, and memories of what Elvis had meant to their parents' generation which made me feel that his death should be noted in church. I realised that it was this combination which made the death of Elvis important to children who knew little about him.

When I raised the subject in church I had three purposes in mind:

1. I felt it was important for the children to know that their parents had enthusiasms just like theirs. Human beings quickly forget the things they feel they have grown out of. I wanted to open up the subject of pop stars for discussion between parents and children. My hope was that in doing this, the subject would cease to be a source of conflict and become a resource for communication.

2. I wanted to take the opportunity to point out that a media superstar is not always everything it appears to be on the posters. At the same time, I wished to underline the thought that some lifestyles which are never written up in lights, like belonging to a church family, having an enduring value and brightness.

3. In many ways, this childrens segment was for the parents. I knew that whether they admitted it or not, the death of Elvis would have been a shock to most of them. Despite this, many of them, especially those who came from rigid and conservative backgrounds, would have difficulty in talking about his death, especially with their families. In many ways, Elvis epitomised for all of us the secular values of our times and, as such, his death was the shaking of the foundations of this particular world-view. In a gentle way, I wanted to say to these adults, 'Hey, even if you completely reject his life style, don't be surprised if you felt a little upset'. And most of all, I wanted to say to them in the childrens address, 'This is an im-

portant subject for you to talk about with your children. It is especially so for those of you who worry that Abba are sweeping your children away. Don't argue with them; share your stories and your own journey through the glossy facade to the getting of wisdom'.

The service had a strange effect on some adults. They did not say very much, although I sensed they were deeply moved. I think that these folk had grown up in an atmosphere of opposition to Elvis, and what he was seen to be standing for. For them, he was a *persona non grata* in their family conversations. But nothing could prevent them from thinking about him. Yet their thoughts about him and all he represented had always been clandestine. I suspected that in the week of his death, their thoughts and feelings were still kept under wraps. To all outward appearances, they were untouched by this event; but they were not. Some, no doubt, felt that people like this had no place in church. Certainly a few seemed shocked or disturbed when I first displayed his picture. I know that some of them felt the same way about Abba yet were unwilling to prevent their children from hanging their pictures above their beds. Such is the world in which we live. If all of life has its place in worship, such influences must be mentioned and reflected on. To ignore them would be to follow the example of the ostrich.

Elvis will only die once, but as sure as night follows day, other pop stars will continue to rise and fall. In our electronically-wired lounge rooms, children will continue to discover entertainers whom they adore and of whom their parents disapprove. There is no end in sight to family differences about unsuitable records and outrageous posters.

In the month prior to writing this chapter, the children of Australia were in the grip of yet another pop fever. The rock group Kiss seized the imaginations of the children from one end of the country to the other. Abba looks positively wholesome in comparison to these painted, fire-breathing incarnations from a horror comic book. For weeks, many children could talk of nothing else. The best efforts of teachers could not drive their influence from the class rooms, nor could the strongest words of parents keep Kiss mementoes and pictures out of their childrens' bedrooms.

During the same period, a second event out of the rock scene brought dismay to many millions across the world; that was the slaying of John Lennon. Like the death of Elvis, this event became a media blockbuster. Everyone knew about it, even the children. In recent years, the combination of John Lennon's recluse-like existence and the esoteric nature of his music meant that, at the time of his death, he was a long way from the attention of most children. Nonetheless, he was not so far away as to leave our children unaffected. They knew he was no ordinary man. He had been a pop star.

And so it will go on. Elvis will only die once but the issues raised by his death will remain. Ministers will continue to ponder whether or not it is appropriate to say anything to children in worship about their pop star heroes or heroines. This question is not about to go away. In fact, there is every indication that via increasingly electronic media, our exposure to super slick and often outrageous pop stars will increase. A possibility this raises is that future children will be even more vulnerable to pop star crushes than children were in the past. I cannot believe that the wisest course is to say nothing. For me, this would be as stupid as to ignore the fact that children go to school. In many ways, this pop world is a kind of school. Unlike other kinds of school, the children flock into this learning arena of their own volition, with their defences down and their antennae closely tuned.

Once the decision is taken to say something, the hardest problem is just what to say. For the people who are sure that the world of entertainment is evil, the answer would be straightforward. All they will need to do is to tell their children periodically that the pop world is corrupt, and of the devil, and that they must keep away from it. To be effective, this kind of counsel would need to be supported by the removal of radio and television sets from the home, or some extraordinarily tight form of censorship. Another problem is that the forbidden apples tend to have the sweetest taste. Consequently, prohibitions of this type may, in the long run, produce in children a stronger than normal craving for exposure to and involvement with the pop world.

Personally, I am not a believer in this approach. As this chapter indicates, I believe we must raise these matters with children in church. As I have said, this is important not only for the children, but also for their parents. However, when it comes to precisely how to do this, I have much to learn. I am not satisfied with the way I dealt with the death of Elvis. Writing it up, it seems that the preacher within me dominated in places where openness would have been more honest and creative. But once again, I was working in an area without models. Nonetheless, I am glad I attempted to tackle this topic, and the experience has encouraged me to continue raising such an important subject.

An explanation of how I proceeded in the two events mentioned above may be of some interest. In the case of Kiss, I attempted nothing at all in church. However, in a childrens holiday activity setting, we dressed young people in Kiss make-up and turned them into clown figures. In this guise, they made fun of Kiss, their make-up, their mannerisms, and their image. I believe that this send-up was helpful to many children in that it demythologised the Kiss image. However, it did little for some of our church elders, who were convinced that we were trying to turn children into Kiss fans; such is the anxiety of adults as they face the latest pop phenomena. This only serves to underline that one important reason for talking about the pop world in church is to help the adults.

Regarding John Lennon's death, I decided to do no more than to make passing mention of it in the childrens segment. However, later in the worship service, I played a portion of a Lennon/McCartney song 'A Long and Winding Road'. Over the latter part of the song, I had recorded an extract from Martin Luther King's sermon 'I Have a Dream'. The sermon that morning was about 'Dreams and Dreamers'. As I mentioned John Lennon in the sermon, I noticed that the older children were paying particular attention.

RESOURCING THE WORSHIP

LITANY

As part of the prayers of intercession, I led a litany for lonely people. In this I used the suggestions previously volunteered by the children and adults. The form of the litany was simple. After each petition, I said, 'Lord, hear our prayer', to which the congregation would reply, 'And let our cry come unto thee'. Here is an example:

> Lord, we pray for people who are lonely because their fame and their riches prevent them from meeting ordinary people.
> Lord, hear our prayer.
> *People:* And let our cry come unto thee.

Lord, we pray for people who are lonely because they are so busy searching for food that they have no time for friendship.
Lord, hear our prayer.
People: And let our cry come unto thee.
Lord, we pray for those who are lonely because they are in prison.
Lord, hear our prayer.
People: And let our cry come unto thee.
Lord, we pray for those who are lonely because they have imprisoned themselves in a prison of selfishness.
Lord, hear our prayer.
People: And let our cry come unto thee.

THE SERMON

I entitled the three-part sermon 'Elvis died because of our sins'.

First, I had the adults cast their minds back to the time they were 18 or 19. I posed the question how they would have reacted at that point in their lives, if someone had offered to make them rich and famous. From there, I led them to wonder what life path any one of us might have followed if, in our early twenties, riches and adulation were heaped upon us.

Second, I put the proposition that pop stars' behaviour and lifestyle reflects what their fans hanker after. Applying this to Elvis, it would mean that he became what his fans wanted him to be. They used him to live out their fantasies and that, finally, it was these same fantasies which imprisoned him. 'How many here today', I asked, 'could deny that at some time and in some way, Elvis had lived out their fantasy or an aspect of a fantasy of theirs?'

Third, the heart of the sermon was an exposition on Jesus' sayings about saving and losing life (Luke 9:23-26).

In my concluding point, I returned once again to the death of Elvis and made the following points. Whatever we thought of him, none of us can stand in judgment on him. Our small scale materialism, our secret hankering after pleasure, or hunger for applause are in God's sight, no different to these same things which we see writ large in the lives of the pop idols of our day. In a dramatic way, Elvis shows us where this road is leading. For our own sake and for the sake of our children, we must wholeheartedly seek that better way of Christian self-giving and to live it with real enthusiasm. In this way, when our children see through the glitter of their pop idols, they will be aware of another kind of radiance which is the life that comes from God.

Chapter 7

Talking about the worst journey in the world

Today, everyone had something to say. I had asked if any of them had ever had something go wrong when they were on a journey. As I often did, I lifted the smallest person to the microphone. He looked at me, but via the microphone, he was talking to the whole congregation. It seemed his parents' car had been bogged in a ditch. He told how he had to wait with his mother whilst his father walked to get help; no small adventure when you are only four. Stories followed one after the other. As usual with children, they were all pretty much to the point. In the space of two or three minutes, we heard about accidents, breakdowns and sleeping in an airport.

It was my turn to share. I told about my worst journey. This was a journey across frozen plains in the United States in a bus whose heating had failed. I recounted how I shivered the miles away and how I thought the end of my nose really would drop off!

'I've heard about a bus journey that is worse than that', I said. 'In fact, some people tell me it's the worst bus journey in the world.' From behind the lectern, I produced a rolled-up poster. Unrolling it, I showed it first to the children and then to the congregation. On the poster was a picture of a small blue bus. 'Do you know why this is the worst bus journey in the world?' I asked. No one knew. 'Does anyone know what this bus is for?' A little girl knew. 'It's the spastic bus.' Soon, everyone had recognised it. Twice every day, blue buses of this kind moved around our neighbourhood, picking up handicapped children and adults, and taking them to schools and special workshops.

Recognition increased the puzzle. At first, the children could not think of any reason why a ride on that bus could be the worst journey in the world. After a pause, a little girl put up her hand. 'I think it might be because all the people who ride on the blue buses are sick.' The answer made sense to a lot of children. Other children told about seeing people in wheelchairs being helped onto the buses. A boy thought he knew. 'Perhaps the wheelchairs roll around in the bus and the people are frightened of getting hurt.' I was able to explain how on the bus, each person and wheelchair had a special place with a safety belt just right for them. 'For people with handicaps, buses like this blue one is just the most comfortable and safest kind of bus to ride in', I explained.

'I don't think you could ever guess why some people tell me riding on these buses is the worst journey in the world. 'You see', I said, 'it has nothing to do with what happens *inside* the bus, it has to do with what happens *outside* the bus.' Turning to the poster, I read the words which were printed alongside the illustration. 'For a spastic, riding on the blue bus is no picnic. It's not much fun being on show, but spastics get used to it. The spastic childrens society provides blue buses, because public transport is inaccessible to spastics. So next time you see a blue bus, have a thought for those inside.' 'Have a thought for those inside', I repeated. 'The trouble is, some people have only unkind thoughts for the passengers in these blue buses. And that is why some handicapped people say that riding on these buses is just horrible.'

I asked did any of the children know what some people did when they saw the blue buses drive by. Some children were looking rather uncomfortable. No one answered. 'They laugh', I said, 'and when the people are getting on the bus, they stop and stare and point. Do you know who it is that laughs most?' The children had all stopped wriggling. 'It's not the adults. It's sometimes the teenagers, but mostly it's the children. Do you believe that?' They said nothing but their eyes told me they believed. 'Well, I think it is that laughter which makes riding around our suburbs in a blue bus the worst journey in the world.'

I asked the children why did people stare and laugh at handicapped people. As I expected, they didn't have an answer. I suggested that after church, the children ask their parents why some children are born handicapped and some are not. 'One thing I do know', I said, 'is that every person who has a handicap is still a person. Just like you and me. Besides, most of us have handicaps of one kind or another. But our handicaps are on the inside, so not everyone knows about them. When you ride the blue bus, everyone knows you have a problem.

'A friend of mine who rides on the blue spastic bus has written a poem about what it's like', I said. 'I would like all of you, boys and girls and mums and dads, to hear it.'

The Blue Bus

Can you imagine riding on the spastic bus?
Because of something you can't help.
As they put you on, you'd like to say,
'Don't blame me, it's not my fault'.
The kids in the street watch us as though we were some kind of show.
To them, it's like going to a circus.
But we spastics have more courage than you think we have.
You've got to have it to ride that blue bus for ten hours a week,
While people stare, and children laugh.

The church was completely quiet. At last, I broke the silence with a question. 'Do you think there is anything we could do to make handicapped people feel better about riding on the spastic bus?' A girl said, 'We could smile at them'. No-one else had anything to say.

'Do you know that Jesus spent a lot of time with people like those who ride on the spastic bus? He was a good friend to them and I am sure that is what he would like us to be. Maybe you will talk with your families or your school class to see if there is anything we can do to help handicapped people feel better about having to ride the blue bus.' Every head nodded.

THE SETTING

My daughter Michelle is physically handicapped. Living with Michelle has raised my consciousness about the predicament of the handicapped. I have felt the hurt of her frustrations and her tears. My anger has been kindled against those who withhold from the disabled the courtesy due to another human being. Like most friends of the disabled, I was at a loss as to what to do about it. An angry confrontation with the particular individual at the time of the discourtesy could be distressing to the disabled person and might further heighten prejudice in the offending party.

Added to this, I had a particular problem. The basis of this was that in many cases, the worst offenders were children. In my work, I spend a large part of my time and energy persuading adults to be open and to learn from children. It is my belief that in many ways, children are angels (messengers) sent from God to point us in the direction of life. And yet, handicapped people often experience them as devils. I know of many incidents in which the disabled have experienced children as instruments of heartless humiliation. As far as I can understand it, there are two strands of influence which encourage the children to behave in this way. One is the 'speckled bird' syndrome. That is to attack anybody whose appearance is different. The second, I suspect, is that the children are reacting to the discomfort which their parents feel in the presence of the handicapped.

Many adults feel deeply threatened by disabled people. They unknowingly pass on to their children vibes which are heavy with anxiety and suspicion. Their children mistakenly read these to mean that they should respond with hostility to the sources of these bad feelings. Their street behaviour is a consequence to this.

I wish I could say that this was not the case with children of church families. But this would be incorrect. My daughter and others tell me that it is not unusual to find that it is the children of the faithful who are the most accomplished tormentors.

I felt that something should be done about this, but indecision as to what to do led to repeated procrastination. I feared that I was so intimately involved with the problem that my emotions would outweigh good sense and make my contribution counter-productive. When my daughter brought home the poster of the blue bus, I saw in it the opportunity I had been waiting for. I looked at the poster for many weeks before deciding how to use it in church. The opportunity presented itself when a committee which had been charged with investigating future directions for church life, asked for time to share some insights with the congregation.

Over the last couple of years, there had been a growing concern that our congregation's ministry to the community around us was more words than action. In a bruised and broken world, the only folk who worshipped with us were those who apparently had been able to be successful in marriage and respectable business; it seemed like our church was a retreat for the happy and the fortunate. Our charter was healing and reconciliation but the people who were in obvious need of this seldom came near us. We began to wonder if one reason why this was so, could be that we were not making it plain enough that they were welcome.

It was in this context that the committee began to think about the handicapped. We knew that there are a large number of persons with handicaps in our community, but there were very few in our church or any church. After investigating the matter further, the committee discovered that none of our buildings gave easy access to handicapped persons. Nor were any of our toilets suitable for use by persons in wheelchairs. The more the committee thought about it, the more it seemed that our buildings were saying to the disabled, 'Not welcome in here'.

Their investigations into the needs of the handicapped caused the members of the committee to examine their own attitudes to disabled people. They unearthed within themselves all kinds of reservations and hesitations. They guessed that many folk in the congregation would have similar inner restraints. The committee knew that this could not be the mind of Christ for the Christian, or for his church. So they did two things:

1. They set about drafting proposals for alterations to the church buildings which would make all our buildings convenient and suitable for the needs of handicapped people. The committee further suggested that once the changes were made, our church should be unambiguous in opening its doors and its organisations to handicapped people and their families.

2. The committee wanted to begin working at changing the attitudes of the congregation. It was for this reason that they wished to speak to the congregation at the time of worship. They decided to do this by sharing the personal experience of one of their number. He would tell the church of his own growth in his appreciation of the needs and potential of the handicapped. This done, he would briefly introduce the committee's practical proposals.

The initiative had my wholehearted support. I felt that the discussion and whatever action followed it must help to chip away at barriers of prejudice and misunderstanding which kept so many up-tight about disabled people. From the point of view of my own agenda, it seemed to me that the day of their presentation would be an ideal day for me to talk about the blue bus. Their comments would, I felt, in some way re-iterate the childrens segment, while the childrens segment would prepare for their contribution. As it turned out, the combination of the two was also of great help to the children. I noticed that all but the smallest children were interested in the committee's presentation. After the worship, many of them were positively enthusiastic about the suggestions that had been made.

On a personal note, I was glad that my daughter was elsewhere for the weekend. If she had been there, she might have felt uncomfortable. Being one of the few people who was obviously handicapped in our church, she could have felt that the service was solely about her. In fact, this was not the case. Also, as she tends to be self-conscious about my use of her writing in public, her absence meant I could use two of her poems, 'The Blue Bus' and 'Perhaps'.

RESOURCING THE WORSHIP

PRESENTATION

The presentation of the committee took fifteen minutes. It comprised three parts. The first was a committee member telling of his inquiries into the needs of the handicapped, and how it had affected him. He related how his contact with handicapped people had opened his eyes to their personhood. The second part was a five minute audio visual. This slide/tape presentation had been put together by the committee. Its content was based on what the committee had seen being done elsewhere to meet the needs of the handicapped. The third part of the presentation was an introduction to the proposals the committee would be bringing before the church.

PRAYER OF CONFESSION

At first, I thought I should conclude the childrens segment with a prayer of confession. After consideration, I rejected this, believing it would have been too heavy on the children. It would have been as though I was heaping on them all the blame for the community's discourtesy towards the handicapped. Consequently, I led the prayer of confession later in the service, and made it quietly clear that it was a prayer for the entire congregation (and not just the children). Some of the themes taken up in the prayer were:

We confess that at times we turn away from sickness and suffering;

that when faced with needy persons, we often prefer to give our money than our love;

that we pretend we are complete and have no need of help from those who seem frail or disabled.

SERMON

My sermon was a brief reflection on Peter and John healing the cripple at the Beautiful Gate (Acts 3:1-10). On that occasion, Peter told the beggar he had no silver or gold to give him but there was something else he could share. I made particular note of Peter's words, 'I will give you what I have'. In respect to the handicapped, I noted that in contrast to Peter and John, today we did have silver and gold to give them. Frequently, we give money and walk away, and behind our backs, our children laugh at the people we do not wish to face. Whereas, all the time handicapped persons need more than our money, they need us. I noted the experience of a number of people who had found that given the chance, disabled persons have much to give. I noted that many folk had found that disabled people have an abundance of life, strength and courage which they are most willing to share.

Prior to the Benediction, I used one of my daughter's poems. I said it applied to everyone in the congregation, whether their disability was on the outside or on the inside.

Life Is Short

Life is short,
We must live it to the full,
Taking the bad times with the good.
Seeing visions,
Dreaming dreams,
And perhaps,
We will never be defeated.

A further note of interest was that the organist for this service was a blind person.

Chapter 8

Talking about my first song

Ian, Lee-Ann and Gaye were all about six years of age. They beamed at everyone in the congregation from their special little platform. Then they glanced at one another, at me, and at the pianist, who smiled back and kept repeating the introduction to the song. In due course, this entrancing trio would recognise the starting note. Finally, a deep breath and they launched into song:

> 'Whisper a prayer in the morning;
> Whisper a prayer at noon;
> Whisper a prayer in the evening;
> It will keep your heart in tune.'

How beautiful they looked, and to every non-critical ear, they sounded beautiful too! The second verse didn't quite flow as rehearsed:

> '— — — in the morning,
> God — — whispers at noon,
> Whisper a prayer in the evening,
> It will keep your heart in tune.'

Obviously, it was not as easy to learn as the first. As they fumbled the lines, the three children turned nervously to one another and to their pianist. Another smile made all the difference, and on they sang. When it was finished, they beamed with the satisfaction of a grand achievement. After all, they had sung a whole song for the very first time in church. In fact, this was the first time ever.

There are those rare times in worship when sacred silence and eloquent words are all surpassed by applause. This was one such occasion, and I led the response. It was as if all the congregation was given permission to feel good about expressing their joy at the contribution of these children. The rhythm of the next five minutes wasn't as I had predicted. The song item by the children had been placed in the liturgy flow as an introduction to my time with the children. Filled with the buoyant mood that prevailed in the worship just then, I moved confidently to weave both the children and their song into the theme. My reasoning, on reflection, was 'it simply felt right'. However, when I have had occasion to work again on this theme with another congregation, the spontaneous inclusions of this particular day are an integral part of the format.

So, back to the three children, basking unabashed in the praise of their congregation. Their debut was over and it was time to sit down. They moved to do so and I interrupted, 'Could you stay just a little while longer? I have some very important things I'd like to talk about with you'. 'Of course', intimated the children. My microphone was a roving one, so taking it in my hand, I moved closer to the trio. 'That was a very fine song that you sang for us', I said, 'and you made a very lovely sound.' All of them smiled, and one of them whispered with pride, 'I know'. I proceeded to have a chat with them. 'How many times did you practise? How did you remember the words? What did it feel like to be asked to sing in church? Were you nervous? How did you feel just now when you finished your song?' As each child indicated their desire to respond, I moved the microphone to pick up that particular little voice. How earnestly they had tackled their practising and how expectantly they had looked forward to this day! I concluded on behalf of all present, 'Thank you for singing to us'. Turning to all the other children who were sitting at the front, I added, 'We love to have you with us in church and it is a special treat when you can take a part in leading us'.

Lee-Ann, Gaye and Ian had not joined the other children on the floor and I began the part I had prepared: 'My First Song'. Rather than stay where I was, I stepped up on the platform that the trio had used and began;

'It is no secret what God can do;
What he's done for others, he'll do for you.
With arms wide open, . . .'

I sang only the chorus, without music but with every action I could remember. 'Do you know that song?' Some of the children did, and there wasn't an adult who didn't. 'That was the first song I sang in my church. Yes, I can remember that day. I wore a new blue dress and a blue ribbon in my hair. I was seven, and so was my friend who sang with me. It was a very special Sunday when our Sunday school presented songs and plays for all the parents and friends in the church. My Sunday school teacher practised us many times. How excited Valerie and I were! I could hardly wait for that day to come. It did, of course, and when the minister announced our names and the name of the song, out we walked right to the very front of the stage.

'The piano played; Valerie started to sing but Pauline didn't. All the words seemed to vanish from my mind. I couldn't remember them at all. Valerie looked at me and she stopped too. I remember wanting to cry and feeling so nervous. The piano stopped and my Sunday school teacher smiled and whispered, "It's alright, we'll start again". This time, the words were there and we sang quite loudly too, as I remember.'

I then explained how important that day was for me, fleshing out each reason with a personal illustration:

Of course, there were mistakes in that first song, but my memories were not of people being cross at me, but of encouraging smiles and interested comments.

I could hardly wait for a time when I could sing, recite, read the Bible or just do anything similar in church again.

My first song was an occasion of feeling I could play a part in my church in a special way.

My first song was a way of growing to know that I belonged to God's family and to him.

I addressed the children, 'Could you turn and face the congregation?' My next question was to the adults. 'How many of you can recall your first song, or a first experience of leading in some way in the life of the church?' Memories had already been nudged in the previous conversations and many raised a hand. The children seemed very impressed that the adults had once had similar experiences.

I summarised in this way: 'That first time at singing or handing out the hymn books is very important, and when we do these same tasks many times over, their value to the life of this congregation does not change. We are all invited to help make church happen.' I looked at the children, 'And you are always included. We take our part because we love God and the special family he has given us'.

Prior to the service, I had planned for one of the elders to come and lead the closing prayer. Before his prayer, he recalled how as a teenage boy he had presented a short talk in his tiny country church, and how very nervous he had been. Shyly he concluded, 'This is the first time since then, that I have said a prayer aloud in church'. He prayed:

> Thank you for the many first times that come because we are part of your family. Thank you for the children and their first song.
> Help us to give our best, not just the first times but every time.
> In the name of Jesus, who knows and loves each one of us. Amen.

THE SETTING

When it comes to children growing up in the Christian faith and Christian church and staying with both in adult life, I have often pondered over the power of the enculturation process. What helps create that sense of belonging to the congregation? What enables us to feel 'in tune' with the liturgical flow? What are the touchstones that influence and inspire commitment to Jesus and his family? When are we most sensitised to this enculturing power?

To my mind, these are issues of great consequence. Although there is not one single dominating influence, I am most enthusiastic about this one: encouraging children to attend worship and giving them opportunity and suitable contexts in which to participate.

It was preparation to lead the worship at a church Birthday Celebration that again stirred and focused my thinking on the subject, and hence resulted in 'Talking about My First Song'.

I was aware that special items from the children had been prepared to complement the order of worship. So, in my mind it was important to talk with the children,

    (a) about their participation, and to encourage and affirm them in it;

    (b) to assure them it was important to everyone and to God;

    (c) to let them see that their parents and friends in the congregation had once, as little children, performed their first job or sung their first song in front of a congregation.

A rich resource was the memory of my own childhood experience as a member of a little country church. My parents did not attend the little church in our home town. However, they did not discourage me from doing so. For the first years, a favourite Sunday school teacher would drive to our house and pick me up. That was when we lived out of town. When we moved in to the township, there was no longer the need for a lift. A good walk about a mile would bring you to the church. Now there wasn't the same impetus any more to go, but still I did.

I remember a very rainy and cold Sunday. I was nine. As far as my family was concerned, this wasn't a day for walking a mile to church. Besides, my mother had scorched my one Sunday school dress. With every good reason, my family proceeded to dissuade me from going. After several minutes of their well intentioned badgering, 'Why do you have to go? Stay home this once', I blurted out, 'I have to go because if I don't, I'll be missed. What's more they need me!' Well, that was that — silence. With scorched dress, off I went to Sunday school and church.

I have no idea on what theological grounds, a nine year old can sustain the reasons given above, but at the time, I felt very sure of both. On reflection, the bond of commitment and belonging were already tied. That event occurred some two years after the occasion of my first song in church.

An incident just prior to this Sunday reaffirmed the direction of my preparation. I was visiting a family in our church. Phillip the youngest boy, eight years old, ran to greet me, excitedly flapping a sheet of paper in front of my face. 'Look, I've been asked to do this!' A Bible reading, some four verses, had been typed on the now soiled and creased paper. 'I'm to practise this every day. I just about know it already. I've been asked to read the Bible next Sunday.' He was bursting with pride and excitement. Then, just for a practice, he read it to me there on the doorstep. 'You'll read it very well, I'm sure, Phillip.' 'Yes', he said, 'it's the first time and I want to do it just right'. Talking to his parents later revealed that Phillip often acted in plays at Sunday school, and reading the Bible in front of his class. But to be asked to read in front of everyone in the church, and as part of the church service, was a very special honour.

Of course, giving a child responsibility in the life of the church need not be the pivotal factor in determining whether that child stays with it or walks away. However, its weighty influence in achieving the former cannot be discounted.

Often, children participating in worship are looked upon as cute and sweet interruptions. Also their presentation is regarded as no more than an item with little relevance to the flow and theme of that Sunday's worship.

There is no denying that our children are like brightly wrapped gifts with their beauty and sparkle. However, we do well to remind ourselves to take their contribution seriously and invite them to share in our own responsibilities and what performing these tasks means to us. For when the children grow out of their cuteness, and become self-conscious about giving items, they could well grow out of the faith, nurture and fellowship of their church, potentially their extended family.

I guess, in many ways, 'Talking about My Song' was intended also as a challenge to the adults. The theme doesn't require a church anniversary or similar celebration. However, for these days, it is likely that special items have been rehearsed. Also, milestone occasions seem to create a greater readiness to remember and reflect upon past journeys and their meaning for the present. Folk are generally more open to joyful expressions of celebration, and sensitive to the spirit of family and 'peopleness' among their number.

When I last used this theme, the minister at the church came up to me and recalled the experience of his first sermon: 'I knocked over the vase of flowers beside the pulpit'.

Our stories are more than anecdotes. They are a valuable source of inspiration and teaching for our children and the whole congregation.

RESOURCING THE WORSHIP

The theme of 'Talking about Something Important' was not so much directly related to the overall worship but as it was modelled in the various segments of the liturgy. I'll explain.

Besides the little children, there were some other firsts for the congregation and some other first timers.

AN ALL-AGE CHOIR

Where you have a resource of good and enthusiastic singers, this is well worth the effort. Although there was a regular adult choir, the addition of teenagers and children was a first. They presented two items.

1. An anthem, the Gloria; one of the brighter, stirring kind;
2. 'For all the saints'; a male soloist sang the first verse, a woman the second, a trio of teenagers the third, and a small group of children sang the fourth. The whole choir joined in for the remaining verses.

This hymn was unannounced and followed the reading of Hebrews 12: 'Let us keep our eyes fixed on Jesus . . .' The combination of that particular reading and the different ages singing each verse was a very powerful message.

AN AUDIO/VISUAL PRESENTATION OF 'FOR ALL THE SAINTS'

On one occasion only, have I added a further layer. If there comes a birthday celebration of some significance in your congregation, it is worth introducing.

One of the members sought out pictorial records of the early church, the particular denominations and the Christian pioneers of Australia. Added to this were slides of the past events and gatherings of their own church family. This required a zealous fossicker, and equipment that could take slides from books and old photographs. The last step was to place these in chronological order and during the first verses, before the whole choir joined in, the slides were flashed on to the wall, changing at seven second intervals.

At the end of the reading from Hebrews, I introduced 'For all the Saints' in this way;

'Let us reflect on the journey of those who have gone before us in faith, those who form this great crowd of witnesses. We will give thanks to God for them and keep our eyes fixed on Jesus.'

OTHER FIRST TIMERS

The elder who led the childrens prayer was not the only first timer. One of those who led the reading had never done so before. A family group took up the offering for the first time.

SERMON

Psalm 26 was set for that day and the text I chose was verse 12: 'I am safe from all dangers; in the assembly of his people I praise the Lord.' (T.E.V.)

I mentioned before, that these special days have more potential for experiment and creativity. Believing that, I began with a monologue as if it was being presented by King David himself, and as if he were addressing the Christian church today.

Although there was much the children could not understand in the sermon, the introduction and the interweaving of both my childhood experience and the encounter with Phillip and his Bible reading were confirmation that this time and this gathering was also for them.

Chapter 9

Talking about 'rude is . . .'

'How many of you have been to sex education sessions this week?' As I expected, most of the children of primary school age put up a hand. I also put up my hand. 'The Stewart family were there', I said. A small girl called out, 'I saw you'. 'And I saw you, Susan', I replied. Looking intently at the children, I asked, 'Do you think it would be alright to talk in church about the things we heard about in those sessions?' The children looked mystified. They were not often silent, but on this occasion, not one of them had anything to say. I directed the same question to the congregation. They were as tongue-tied as the children, and looked decidedly more uncomfortable. If I was not mistaken, some had stiffened in their seats.

Answering my own question, I said, 'Do you know, in church you can talk about anything at all. God made us as we are and he is interested in every part of our lives'. I went on to say how some people seemed to have the idea that you should never talk in church about people's bodies or about love between men and women. They thought that these things were rude or nasty and not to be talked about by nice people, especially nice church people. 'That's not the way the Bible thinks about it', I said. 'And seeing that's the case, why don't we have a little talk about these things today, here in church?' The children looked interested. Most of the adults looked apprehensive.

In my estimate, the subject was too loaded, especially for the adults, to be talked about in my usual question and answer style. My guess was that whatever a child said, some nervous adults would chuckle. The child who had spoken would feel laughed at and the 'matter of fact' tone I wished to bring to the subject would be lost.

To avoid this, I had the adults turn where they were sitting, and make groups of threes or fours. I asked them to discuss in these groups what role if any our congregation should play in helping with our childrens sex education.

I sat down on the sanctuary steps and gathered the children close around me. 'What did you think of the sex education sessions?' I asked. 'Dumb', said one boy, who acted tough under all circumstances. Other children had different opinions. Most had found them interesting, and a few children said nothing. Our conversation lasted no more than three minutes. On my return to the lectern, there was no debriefing. I told the adults that they would have opportunity to share their opinions at the next session of our adult study.

'What is rude?' I asked the children. Before giving them a chance to answer, I produced from behind the lectern three pictures. To help the congregation, many of whom would have difficulty in seeing them, I briefly described each picture. One was the picture of naked Aboriginal children playing at the edge of a waterhole. The second was that of a handicapped person poking out his tongue. The third was a spectator at a football match throwing a can at a player. I asked the children, 'Do any of these pictures show someone being rude?' For a moment or two, children giggled and poked each other. Then cautiously they began to express their opinions. In the end, every picture was named by someone as being rude. The one about which there was most consensus was the picture of the spectator throwing the missile.

When the children had had their say, I remarked how interesting it was to see that what was rude to one person was not rude to another. 'That's the way it is around the world', I said. Then I made a comment about each picture. Concerning the picture of the Aboriginal children, I told of one of my Sunday school teachers who used to say that only rude people go without clothes. I went on to recount how we know that many Aboriginal people who never wore clothes were much better people than many white people who wore lots of clothes. Of the picture of the person sticking out his tongue, I noted that usually people would think that that was a rude expression. But I was able to point out that with this person, things were different. I explained about the handicap which made him stick out his tongue every time he was excited. Looking at the picture of the spectator throwing the can, I pointed out that this person had all his clothes on. As well as this, although he looked cross, he certainly was not pulling a face. However, as we could all see, what he was doing was very unfriendly and unfair. I asked the children to think some more about what is rude, or when is a person being rude. I suggested they should discuss this with their parents after church.

Coming back to the sex education sessions, I said, 'Some people will say rude is people with no clothes on, or anything to do with sex. Well, sometimes it may be; but it needn't be. Like the three pictures we looked at today, when you understand about people, you realise that some things which might look rude are not rude at all, and some actions which might not look too bad are very rude. Certainly, in the family of Jesus, we want you to understand about the wonderful way God has made you. There is nothing about the way he made us which in itself is rude or that we need be ashamed of. In conclusion, I prayed this prayer:

> 'Lord, we thank you that you made us boy and girl, man and woman. We thank you that each of us is special and beautiful in our own way. Help us to understand our bodies and to keep them strong and beautiful for your sake and for others.
>
> Help us, Lord, to enjoy and respect the bodies of others, and in your right time, may our bodies produce all the energy and life you want them to.
>
> Save us from judging people by their appearance.
>
> Teach us what rudeness is and keep us from it.
>
> In the name of Jesus, who loves us, each one, we ask this prayer. Amen.'

THE SETTING

Many Australian primary schools have specialists in sex education visit every two or three years. Over a period of a week, these specialists lead evening sessions for parents and children at graded levels to cover all the students in the school. At the time of the episode detailed above, I was minister in a village situation. In our small community, there was a phenomenal attendance at the sex education sessions. It seemed that for the entire week, the subject was a big deal for every child and the adults related to them. I can still visualise these serious-looking adults, with overawed children sitting beside them, listening intently as a most pleasant man talked about and illustrated what for many of them had previously been unmentionable. Everything was dealt with in most excellent taste, though it was rather clinical, and all of it totally secular. Thinking on this experience which my family had shared with so many other church families, I realised that in church we had never even broached the subject of physical relationships between men and women. It would be understandable, I reasoned, if our children were to think that sex was something about which our church had nothing to say. So it was because of a community-based education event that I felt compelled to raise the matter in church.

In a suburban congregation, it is not likely that a situation exactly parallel to this will arise. Children will be attending different schools and no one school program would have this level of impact on a church or a community. On the other hand, I know it is the practice of some congregations to sponsor these sessions for their own families. And it is possible that other kinds of events could create an atmosphere in which an initiative similar to the one outlined would be advantageous to all.

Here, I am thinking of things like a widely viewed sex instructional film on television, a neighbourhood rape, or a local flood of pornography. If, for any reason, the subject of sex has been thrust before your children with heightened pressure, then that is an excellent time to attempt some 'in church' dialogue.

We should not be too patient in waiting for the right time to raise these matters. If the opportunity does not come, then we should plan to make some foray into these areas on our own initiative. Warrant enough for doing this is because the Bible is not shy about such matters. Another reason is that we live in a sex-saturated society. Our children are not blind, and there is plenty of evidence to show that even young children are being profoundly influenced by the sex-charged atmosphere of our day. In church, our children hear us talk of and pray about life, from birth to death. However, in most congregations, they will never hear any positive reference to human sexuality. Within our sanctuaries, it is almost as though we pretend that our sexual nature does not exist. It seems to me that the total silence on this subject in church may be as confining and negative to our children as the over-emphasis it receives in the world. How can this situation best be changed? Clearly, instruction and discussion in a Christian atmosphere would help. But classes are not enough. If our sexual nature is truly a God-given gift, we must be able to speak of it affirmatively in the holy hour of worship. It is there that we must break the silence. Our children need to see that this part of our nature is as much a gift from God as any other aspect of life. It is my conviction that an early realisation of this will give a perspective which will form a defence against the propaganda which seeks to exploit and distort this powerful life stream.

In the years since the episode described in this chapter, I have not repeated it in its entirety. The principal reason for this is that I have never again had that unique situation which was created by the community education sessions. However, I have continued to deal with the topic in church, but generally in two parts and on two separate occasions.

The easiest to manage is the second part, which starts with the question 'what is rude?'. In actual fact, this question inevitably raises the subject of human sexuality. It has always provoked useful 'in church' interaction and 'after church' family conversations. It also allows me to note the Bible's positive view of our sexual nature.

The first part of this segment is more difficult. It approaches questions of sexuality head-on, and my hunch is that in most congregations, both children and adults would be too uncomfortable to handle it. It seems to me that to carry this one off, what is needed is a unique situation (similar to this chapter) or an atmosphere of great trust and warmth as in a family camp.

RESOURCING WORSHIP

More than most subjects, I have had trouble relating this topic to the worship experience. In cases like this, I try to avoid forcing an unnatural relationship. Nonetheless, even when nothing more is said, it is my perception that the segment does make a difference to the entire service. It is as though I give young and old in the congregation fresh evidence that what we are about here is real life, your life. Their response to this seems to be to sit up and take notice of the liturgy of the day in all its parts.

Here are some specific ways in which the meaning of this particular childrens segment has been expanded in the following flow of worship.

A DANCE INTERPRETATION OF 1 CORINTHIANS 13.

This required a deal of preparation by a talented young woman dancer and a reader/producer. The reader/producer selected a piece of music which was suitable to accompany the reading and to accommodate the dance. In the service, the reading, dance and music were a beautiful whole. The music and the dance added an eloquent, extra dimension to the inner feeling of the passage. Nor was there any need for me to draw attention to the fact that the dance was an acted parable which gathered meaning through the beauty of the female body. The Bible passage was my text for the day, and although not making much of them, the conversations with the children and the danced Bible readings were clearly the backdrop against which the sermon was preached.

TESTIMONY OF PREJUDICE:

On another occasion, when I had talked with the children about 'Rude Is . . .', a lay person who had been a refugee led the pastoral prayer. Prior to leading this prayer, she briefly mentioned three unhappy incidents from her early years in Australia. She spoke of times when she was treated rudely because of her accent, her clothes and her inability to understand the language. Her prayer took up the theme of the plight of the refugees around the world and especially those who were now the strangers in our midst.

A SERMON ON THE ESSENTIALS OF THE GOSPEL

On a separate occasion, this sermon followed my conversation with children about 'Rude Is . . .'. The person who gave the address was one who had a lifelong association with overseas mission. He started by talking about the standards which missionaries used to force upon those who would follow Jesus. As he gave examples of what the missionaries used to make the natives do and wear in the name of Christianity, the congregation was amused and saddened in turn. 'Earnest missionaries did these things', he said, 'because they had a mistaken idea of what rude is'. He talked of the dismay which many missionaries felt when they realised that Western missionaries had really been the rude ones by the way they forced their standards on the native peoples. He then went on to tell how missionaries who were willing to listen, learned that these new Christians from other cultures had much to teach them about the true meaning of the gospel. His sermon concluded with a plea to everyone, young and old, to refrain from judging those who are different, and to seek God's help to be loving in all our relationships.

In conclusion, I wish to say that I am more than usually unsatisfied with my approach to this subject. The danger of articulating or implying value judgments on other people or their views is very great. Also, any discussion on this subject can easily become a snicker session for children and adults. When this happens, it tends to be counter-productive to the entire exercise. The thing I do feel right about is that I do try to talk about these things in church. I am sure there must be better ways of doing it. In this chapter, I have set out my efforts as an example to be improved upon.

Despite my misgivings, it seems that my attempts in this area have all had some positive value. There have been no complaints from either parents or children. On the contrary, parents, Sunday school teachers and club leaders tell me that their children have been more willing to discuss matters sensibly after my session in church. It is my suspicion that this is only half of the story. I suspect that, in many cases, it was the adults who were most helped, and that they were the ones who were now willing to talk.

Chapter 10

Talking about who makes wars

Instead of joining me at the front of the church, twelve of the children went out into the church porch. Some children looked perturbed but I was not. This is exactly how we had arranged it at our rehearsal on the previous day. From my briefcase, I produced copies of the last week's newspapers. I showed the front page of each of these to the children and the congregation. It had been one of those weeks of international threat and counter-threat. The headlines on most editions used large type to spell out bad news.

'Do you ever get worried about the news in the papers?' I asked. As I had expected, the children were silent. I had noticed before that children have to feel at ease before they will admit to having any worries at all. I smiled and waited. Before long, one of the older children raised her hand. 'I worry about the people who haven't enough food', she said. By the time I had relayed her comment to the congregation, another child had a worry to share. In all, four children told of their worries. Two of them said they were worried about another world war. As will be seen, I both expected and hoped to get this answer. I was not in much doubt that it would come because other conversations with children had made me aware that this fear is in the heart of many children.

I admitted that a fear of war was something which worried me too. I went on to tell a story from my childhood. 'After school, I would often visit my school friend's home. We would do our homework together and sometimes I would stay for dinner. On a couple of occasions, we had a rice dish. I noticed that whenever rice was on the table, my friend's father would push it away. Not only that, but it seemed that he could not bear to watch us eat it. When we began to eat, he would suddenly get up and, with an angry look on his face, leave the room. I asked my friend what was it about rice which made her father so angry. She told me that for three years he had been a prisoner in a Japanese prison camp. It seems that every day for three years, rice was his only food. Now, whenever he saw rice, he thought of the prison and the Japanese. My friend told me that her father grew angry every time he thought of the Japanese. That was why he used to get upset whenever he saw rice on the table.'

It made me think how terrible war must be. It was very confusing because at school, we were told that the Japanese and the Australians were starting to be friends. About that time, I began to wonder why do wars start and who starts them. 'Do you ever wonder that?' I asked. Children nodded. Turning to the congregation, I said, 'I am sure that everyone here has, at one time or another, asked that question. Well, with the help of some children, I have tracked down some of the terrible people who start wars. This morning we are going to show you just who they are.' This was the cue for action and the children in the porch were ready.

At the back of the church, a kettle drum began to beat out a menacing rhythm. People turned around to see a line of twelve figures processing down the aisle. The twelve were arranged in pairs. First came a child with a cowboy-style mask. This child carried a piece of wood which was shaped like a rifle. This was held as though ready for combat. The second person in each pair wore a black hood and carried a large placard. When they reached the front of the church, they turned and faced the congregation. At the front stood the gunmen and behind them the hooded figures with their placards held high.

Each placard carried one blunt statement. For the sake of the children who could not read and members of the congregation who could not see, I read aloud the message printed on each card:

I don't like you, get out of my way.
I want what you've got, hand it over.
I am better than you, and I am going to prove it.
I'm going to get even with you.
Follow my suggestions or else.
I am going to rescue you, whether you like it or not.

'Have you ever heard a person say something like what is written on any one of these placards?' I asked. Heads nodded. 'Tell us about it.' With a roving microphone, I went to the children who indicated they had something to say. We heard of confrontations at school, fights on the way home, and harsh words between siblings. 'Sometimes', I said, 'I have heard words just like that within my own head.

They have come straight out of my own heart. Maybe you have had a similar experience'. 'Do you know what?' I said, 'That's why people go to war. The sentences on the placards are the kind of reasons which make people want to fight someone else'.

I turned to the hooded placard bearers. 'So here are the people who start wars. Let's see who they are.' I moved down the row and unmasked each of the children. As I did so, the gunmen guarding that person lowered the gun and sat with the other children on the floor. Behind each frightening hood was a child known to the congregation. As I removed each mask, I read the message of their placard once again. After I did this, each child lowered its placard to the floor. Then I introduced him or her to the congregation.

'Do you know what this means?' I asked. 'If these really are the reasons why people go to war, then there is a little bit of "the war maker" in all of us. That means if we became very powerful and thought we could get whatever we wanted, then we could be the people who start wars. Just think of that. None of us wants a war, but if we let these "war maker" feelings rule our lives, then it's just possible that you or I could start a war. Isn't that terrible?' The children agreed.

'I know that all of you want just the opposite to that.' I explained that on the day before, I had asked the children who were to carry the placards to think out their answer to an important question. That question was 'What is your hope for the future of the world?' I moved to the first child and held the microphone close to her mouth. The answer she had thought out was clear and concise. She wanted to live in a world of peace, not at war. In similar fashion, each child made their own statement of hope. As the children shared their hopes, I was conscious of the warm response which was forthcoming from the congregation.

To close the segment, the children who had held the placards led the congregation in a prayer of confession. It was to be, I explained, an 'eyes open' prayer. One by one, each of the children moved to the lectern. There, they once again held their placard high and read a brief prayer which was based on the wording upon it. This is how it went:

'God, forgive us when we don't like another person.' The congregation's response (led by me) was: 'Amen'. This child moved to one side and the next child stood at the lectern with placard held aloft. 'Lord, forgive us when we want that which belongs to another.' Again, the people responded: 'Amen'.

After each child had led their prayer, they lowered their placard and, taking them to the front of the church, laid them down flat at the foot of the cross.

THE SETTING

Ever since starting to work with children, I have been aware that some of them worry about the possibility of another war. I believe that, in recent years, the number of children who are conscious of this fear is on the increase.

For me, it was a conversation with a friend that brought the matter to a head. She is a school teacher in a suburban school. Each suitable school day, she usually takes her class into the playground for some physical activity. Recently, as they were enjoying some games, a rather large plane flew low overhead. Immediately, three of her children broke off from the game and ran into the school building. Irritated at this unexpected behaviour, she followed the children into the school. To her surprise, she found that all three of them were crying. It took her some moments to calm them down. She noted that their cries were not the usual cries of naughty children. Finally, the source of their tears came blurting out: 'The Russians are coming to drop bombs on us'. It was then that she realised their tears had been tears of fear. When my friend told me this story, she shook her head in wonder. 'Who could believe that children in peaceful, far-flung Australia could be stirred to tears at the sight of an aeroplane overhead?'

Newspapers and radio have always lived on sensation. But the worst they could do was to heap word on word. Television operates out of the same priorities, but to the words it adds moving pictures in full colour. If a bloody battle is fought out anywhere on the globe, more than likely it will be seen in our lounge-rooms within twenty-four hours. Adults may find this interesting viewing; it is more than that for the children. Wars and rumours of wars may unsettle adults, but they terrify some children, and frighten a great many more. Given our unstable world and the development of technology, there is every likelihood that the flow of vivid coverage of violent scenes will increase. In fact, we may not be far from the situation in which the 'live coverage of battles as they happen' will be with us. No doubt if this happens, television stations and sponsors will carefully analyse its rating potential. Who knows but live coverage of a real war may come to challenge sport as a TV draw card.

All this may be abhorrent to us, but what can we do about it? Short of withdrawing ourselves from the world, there is little we can do to stop the visual images of violence and war surrounding our children. However, we do know that children who live within a complex of stable and supportive relationships can remain emotionally unscathed by these outside influences. For this reason, the local church must ceaselessly work at being a loving, extended family for all of its children.

One other way in which the church can help is by talking with children in church about the violence in the world which they see on the television news. On the day described here, I attempted to tackle the question of war from the basic question of the goodies and the baddies. Children are drawn towards the black and white politics of the goodies (us) against the baddies (whoever we are fighting). It was my intention to make a start at answering the difficult question 'Who starts wars?' In doing this, I wanted to lift the question of wars and war-making above the level of the good 'us' and the bad 'them'. Also, I felt most strongly that we must constantly do all we can to remind Christians of all ages of the commission which Christ gave to all his followers to be peacemakers. Our efforts in this respect will have most effect if we begin commending this beautiful role to our children while their hearts are tender.

PREPARATION FOR THE WORSHIP

To help prepare this segment, I had two Sunday school classes meet with me on the day before the service. After discussion, the children and I decided upon the six war-like phrases. Some of the children wrote out the signs and nailed the cards to pieces of wood, so that the placards could be held high. Other children worked on the hoods. Six grocery bags were cut to fit and painted black. We rehearsed the way things would happen in church next day. Six children were the 'demonstrators' and these wore the black grocery bags and held the placards. Another six children were the bodyguards for the demonstrators. They wore handkerchief masks and carried toy rifles. Each bodyguard practised walking a few paces in front of a demonstrator up the centre aisle of the church. Each pair was to march in time to the beat of a drum. The drummer was one of the children who happened to be in a school band. He was to stand at the back of the church and his drum beats would be the cue for the entry of all the rest.

RESOURCING THE WORSHIP

THE READING

The New Testament reading was the story of the Good Samaritan (Luke 10:29-37). This reading was introduced as an example of the attitudes which Jesus wanted to see in all of us. The reading was presented by another Sunday school class. Whilst the teacher read the story, the class mimed it out before the congregation. Carefully chosen, recorded background music heightened the dramatic quality of the reading.

THE PRAYERS OF INTERCESSION

These were led by a lay preacher who had been in the armed services in the Second World War. Before leading the prayer, he made brief mention of his wartime experience and the pain and grief it had brought into his own life. The prayer included a number of petitions for peace. These included petitions for international peace, peace within our country and peace in our homes.

THE SERMON

I commenced the sermon with my friend's story of the children and the low-flying aeroplane. Throughout the sermon, I referred to the placards carried by the children. In the concluding point of the sermon, I talked about God's hopes and ours. Here, I reminded the congregation of the hopes the children had shared earlier in the service. Immediately prior to the Benediction, I prayed this prayer:

> 'Dear God, we ask that your spirit of love and forgiveness may enter our hearts. Help each of us, young and old, to be peacemaking people.'

At this point, I invited the congregation to pray for anyone about whom they were feeling angry or resentful. After about a minute of silence, I led the congregation in the Benediction.

There were two other things we thought of doing but did not, because of lack of preparation time. As these ideas may be of use to someone else, we share them here.

The children who were to carry the placards were going to condense their 'hope statements' into a few words. The idea was that they write these on another card of the same size as their placards. After the Benediction, I was to ask the congregation to remain standing. The placard children were then to pick up their placards from in front of the Communion table. Using paper clips, they were to fix their 'hope statements' over the face of the war-like statements. (They may have needed a couple of adults to help them with the mechanics of this.) Holding their 'hope statements' high, they would then precede me out of the church.

Our other thought was that we could once again use the kettledrum during this exit procession. Only on the exit, the mood of the playing should not be menacing but jubilant. To achieve this effect, one of our young people who was a capable flute player was to play a bright and hopeful melody which the drum could accompany.

Chapter 11

Talking about
a day for giving away treasures

No-one else but children could have thought it to be treasure. Comic books, slightly used dolls, very used toy cars, roller skates, a bed lamp with a Disney shade, a surf board and much more. Their owners sat there, each filled with pride in their possession, and above all, pleased with themselves. The goods they held had one thing in common. They had all been purchased by the children at the church fête which had taken place the day before. On the previous Sunday, I had invited the children to bring to church on the next Sunday, one bargain they had bought for themselves at the fête. Looking at the children who sat around the lectern, I could see that at least half the children had taken up my suggestion.

I asked the children with the treasures to stand holding their treasures, so that the congregation could see them. The rest of the children sat before them, looking on in wonder. I walked along the line talking to the children and where necessary, holding up or describing their treasure. Each child had something to say about their prize possession. Some pointed out cracks or chips, others just how they would use their new possession, and a couple of commercially minded people insisted on telling me how much their article had cost. The second last person was holding a book. When I came to her, a child who was sitting on the floor suddenly started calling out. I couldn't quite grasp what she was saying, so I called her forward. She took the book from its new owner, opened the cover and handed the open book to me. Inside the front cover, a name was written. It was her name. She had been trying to tell me that the book used to belong to her. She was the one who had given it to the fête. Once I realised this and had made it clear to everyone, she was content to go back to her seat on the carpet.

The girl's action stirred a new line of thought in me, and I decided to go along with it. After sitting all the children down around the lectern, I asked, 'Would any of you like to tell us about something you gave to the fête?' In the next couple of minutes, a number of children stood with me and told of toys and books which they had donated. Some were quite off-hand, but this wasn't the case with all. For a couple, it was clear that it had been quite a struggle to let a particular thing go from their possession.

After the sharing had finished, I asked what they thought about giving things to the fête for nothing, and then paying money to buy other things which used to belong to other people. It was quite clear to one girl. 'It's not fair', she said, 'you ought to be able to just swap'. Just as quickly, another girl said, 'Then the church wouldn't get any money'. Other comments took up either one of these two points of view. It might have developed into quite a debate, if I had not interrupted. 'It's not just children who have different ideas about these things', I said, 'the adults in your church family do not agree either.' At this point, I had planned to commence small group discussions. The children's comments about how hard it could be to give something away, reminded me that there was something I should say first. Looking particularly at the children, I said, 'I want to thank everyone, children and adults, who gave anything to our fête. Your gifts helped to make the day the great success it was'.

I asked the children to sit in the congregation with adults other than their family. 'That is', I said, 'unless you really want to sit with your parents'. I asked the members of the congregation to turn and make groups of about five. Wherever possible, these small groups were to include a child or children. The discussion task I set was this:

First, they should introduce themselves and then discuss two questions.

1. What did they like best about the fête?
2. What did they like least about this event?

In all of this, they were to be sure to let everyone have their say, including the children. Over the next three minutes, the church was a hubbub of discussion.

The discussion was concluded with a brief plenary session. Starting with the first question, I asked if a man would share his view. This accomplished, I asked a woman to do the same, then a teenager and then a child. I used the same procedure with the second question. By the end of this session, a cross section of the generations in our church had expressed a variety of opinions.

Despite the hard work of the fête, it was obvious that on this morning, most people were buoyed up by its success. This meant that even the 'liked least' comments tended to be light-hearted, rather than totally negative or sour.

As the people shared, I wrote on my pad the main points of their contributions. To conclude this segment, I led a litany based on their comments. I interspersed the 'likes' and the 'did not likes' back-to-back. With some of the comments, I had to add some interpretive comment to make them suitable for this prayer form. Here are some examples:

> Lord, we admit that the fête tired us out.
> We thank you that we found strength enough to bring it to completion.
> Lord, hear our prayer;
> *People:* And let our cry come unto thee.
>
> Lord, we thank you, that as we worked together, we felt we belonged together.
> Lord, hear our prayer;
> *People:* And let our cry come unto thee.
>
> Lord, we feel sorry that for so long we have thought of little else other than this event. Open our eyes that we might see your will for us.
> Lord, hear our prayer;
> *People:* And let our cry come unto thee.
>
> Lord, we are glad that so many people seemed happy to buy the things we had made. Help us always to give our best in all that we do.
> Lord, hear our prayer;
> *People:* And let our cry come unto thee.

THE SETTING

This took place in a small closely-knit congregation numbering about 50 adults and about 40 children. Most of the adults ranged between 30 and 40 years of age; the majority of the children were below eleven years. The small group discussion technique was not new to the congregation, but it was by no means a weekly event. Up till then, inclusion of children in adult groups was an occasional thing.

During the preceding year, the fête had dominated the life of the congregation for more than three months. Financial considerations within the parish at that time made it imperative that the fête be a financial success. Consequently, it was given priority at all levels, and preparing for the fête affected every member and organisation in the church.

The fête was a multi-faceted activity. In the account in this chapter, the children showed purchases which they had made from the second-hand goods stall. But this was only one aspect of the trading at the fête; many persons had been working for months preparing new items to be sold. In the two weeks before the fête, this work built up to such a pitch that it dominated the home life of many church families. On the last few days before the event, many harassed and hassled people mumbled in my ear 'never again'.

For the church folk, the day of the fête turned out to be one of mounting euphoria. The church grounds looked fabulous, people came in great numbers, money rolled in, and the grumbles of yesterday were forgotten. At the end of the day, the church folk had worked themselves to a standstill, but good will abounded on all sides. Clearing up, the sense of weariness took second place to the feeling 'wasn't it wonderful' and 'all the effort had been worth it'. People who had never before thought of our church as a family, felt it to be one on that day.

Nothing caused more controversy in the life of that small congregation than the fête. Some people were total and unwavering enthusiasts. The singlemindedness of their enthusiasm gave reason to suspect that in their view organising fêtes was what church life was all about. These folk loved every aspect of the fête. From the first preliminary notice to the final clean up of the church grounds, they were in their element. Many others did not see it this way. There were those who resented the way it took over the life of their organisation. Others hated the constant talk about the fête and the fund-raising emphasis that accompanied it. During the pre-fête build-up, people who were inexpert or uninterested in handcrafts or the domestic skills of sewing and cooking, felt uncomfortable or even guilty. It worried me because for twelve weeks, we seemed to be thinking and working for ourselves only. Our almost total preoccupation with our own survival seemed to be dreadfully unhealthy. The saying of Jesus about 'saving and losing life' (Matthew 10:39) made me shudder.

Like all good controversies, there was something reasonable which could be said on both sides. From my point of view, I noted that the children really became involved in this event, and through it, with the rest of the congregation. They were with us from the initial preparation to the final cleaning up. For some aspects of the fête, they bore total responsibility. For instance, they looked after their own second-hand toy stall. Many children made cookies and candy, and sold it on their own stall. Others worked for months preparing handcrafts. On the day, you could not have kept the children away if you had paid them. This was their day when they did their bit to help their church.

In a similar way, the fête gave all kinds of adults something to do. Certainly, a few stalwarts produced a huge amount, but many people contributed a little. Folk we hardly knew wanted to make a contribution to our fête. In bringing their goods, they also brought themselves and so we came to know them. For some individuals and a few families, this was their first real step into the church.

I also noted that some men who were real sideline sitters came to life when they saw there was something they could do. And for all of us, it was a good thing to see our fellow worshippers in another setting. We discovered much about the people we met with on Sundays. We learnt of enthusiasms, skills and artistic abilities. Somehow, the people of the church were more three-dimensionally human after the fête.

On the day of the fête, our church looked like a village green and our congregation felt like a community. On the evening of the fête, I had to acknowledge that the success of the day had swept all objections before it. For a time, controversy could be stilled, but I knew it would re-appear next year. The questions raised before this fête would continue to be of central importance to the lfe of the church and the debate would go on. As minister, it would be my responsibility to try once again to bring a theological perspective to the issues.

Ross Snyder, the great American Christian educator had taught me that Christians should celebrate milestones. By a milestone, he meant every group task which had been completed or had been brought to a significant stage of development. His view was that this milestone should be celebrated even when the result was less than might have been hoped for; even if the project had created controversy, even when its accomplishment was likely to be only a temporary victory. In Snyder's view, if any group of people had shared a journey of commitment together up to the completion of a phase of their objective, the arrival at that point was a milestone. No matter how it had worked out, this shared experience was to be remembered and examined for the meaning that could be found within it, and then to be celebrated.

It was thoughts of this kind which made me feel that whether spending three months on the fête had been for the good or ill of church life, it must be remembered and celebrated in worship. More than anything else I could think of, the fête had been a journey shared by the whole congregation. Enthusiastically or grudgingly, we had all made some commitment to it, and had worked together to bring it to a conclusion. Whatever the future held, whether it be a long line of fêtes or never again, this one fête had to be brought into focus in worship.

Events like the fête come and go in the life of most congregations. Sometimes similar energies are focused around a building project, or it may be a fund raising effort for famine relief; or a commitment to give practical and financial support to a local worthy cause. In a sense, it does not matter what it is that brings the people together, if it unites a large part of your church family around one single enterprise, then it is something which should be celebrated in worship. If it is a project which will be completed in a reasonable time, then the celebration should happen at the conclusion of the venture. If it is something which will or could stretch on for years, then it should be celebrated as stages on the way are completed. The rider I would add to this, is that if it involves the children of the parish (and every project should) then the celebration should include them and probably, as in this case, start with them.

Some things which the church calls celebrations are dreary affairs. A speech is made, a sermon is preached, a prayer is read, a slightly suitable hymn is sung and the celebration is over. Snyder always stressed that something of the essence of the enterprise should be brought into the celebration. Objects, which in the project had been the nuts and bolts of the venture, can in worship become clues to the deeper meaning of the enterprise, symbols loaded with spiritual meaning. To enable the meaning to grow, opportunity has to be given within the celebration for personal interaction with the signs and symbols of the shared journey. The meanings which arise out of the celebration will at times surprise everyone. It may be more than was expected. It is because of this possibility that the meaning of a fête may lead the congregation to a commitment to building a caring church family. Without the celebration of the event in worship, it is just as likely to lead to nothing more than the paying off of a few debts or the purchase of cushions for the pews.

RESOURCING THE WORSHIP

As can be seen, this childrens segment grew to take more than seven minutes in the service. I allowed this to happen because I sensed that the issues raised by the children were alive for everyone. I saw it as my task to help channel the energy that was stirred back to the contemplation of the worth and purpose of God which was the primary reason for our gathering.

THE OFFERING

I led the offertory prayer prior to the taking up of the offering. At the conclusion of the reception of the offering, as the stewards brought the offering forward, they were accompanied by other people. This other group, which included children, young people and adults, each held something in their hands. After I had placed the offering plates on the communion table, I approached these additional people. One at a time, I took from each of them the object they were holding and showed it to the congregation. I explained the object only when it was necessary to do so. Most things were self-explanatory and all of the objects had been important components in the success of the fête. After displaying each object, I placed it on the communion table. The articles included a pot of home-made jam, a cake, a picture painted by a member of our congregation, a wooden toy, a plant potted and ready for sale, a hand-sewn apron, a decorative plaque made by a child, and the minute book of the fête committee.

When these had been placed on the table, the people who had carried them returned to their seats. A member of the fête committee led a prayer, thanking God for the many talents he had given to the members of our congregation. As she did this, she mentioned each of the items on the communion table as being representative of yet other skills.

THE SERMON

I preached on Paul's words in Romans 12:1-13, paying special attention to what he had to say on gifts. From time to time, by way of illustration, I referred to the objects on the communion table.

THE BENEDICTION AND DISMISSAL

Prior to the Benediction, I had the people who had brought the fête symbols come forward to the front of the sanctuary. One by one, I took each item from the table. Before I gave each item back to the person who had presented it, I held it high and said, 'Use the skills which this represents to the glory of God and to extend his loving purposes within our world'. After the Benediction, the people bearing these symbols preceded me as I left the church.

Chapter 12

Talking about when people go away

This congregation had a time of fellowship as a regular segment in worship. Folk would be asked to turn to a neighbour, introduce themselves and chat informally about things that were on their mind. Today, I had directed the line of conversation for their fellowship time. I asked them to talk about a move that they had made from another town or suburb, or a move a neighbour or friend had made. I asked them to share a glad or sad thing that they could remember about either of these experiences. Children and adults alike contributed to the buzz of conversation. It was clearly a help to the children to have a special subject to talk about.

At the end of the fellowship segment, I asked the congregation to indicate who among them had made a recent move that was difficult. Who among them faced such a move? A surprising number of hands was raised in response to this question, at least half a dozen, in my estimation. I then invited the children forward as was the regular practice.

Julie immediately came and stood on the riser at my side, exactly as we had planned. 'I've asked Julie to help me with this part of the worship. As many of you know, Julie is new to our church. She arrived only a few weeks ago. When I visited Julie's house, I asked her were there three things that to other people may not seem worth very much, but that she couldn't possibly leave behind in her recent move. Julie had no trouble selecting three items. I'm very glad for you to meet Julie and to see what we brought from her bedroom.'

Despite her nervousness, she beamed at me. I put a hand on her shoulder and moved the microphone over close to her. 'Julie, could you show us what you have?' One at a time, she held high a broken plastic doll, a wrinkled and torn swimming pennant, and a drawing done in crayon. As she did so, I described each item for those who perhaps could not see as clearly as others.

I proceeded to ask Julie these questions:

'Julie, what was it about these three things that wouldn't let you leave them behind even though they look rather old?'

Julie responded readily. 'The broken doll, that is from my penfriend. Well, she was my penfriend, we don't write any more but I like to remember her and the doll is all the way from England.'

I picked up the swimming pennant. Julie continued, 'That's from when I was learning to swim. I didn't think I was going to make it and I came third. I felt very good that day so I wanted to keep it'.

The third item was the crayon drawing. 'Is this the house you lived in?' 'No, it is a drawing of the house I lived in before the last house. I really liked that house.'

'Julie, what were some of the things that looked just as old as this but you had no trouble leaving behind?'

'Oh, I threw away many broken toys and lots of drawings.'

'What made those different from the ones you brought today?'

'Well, I couldn't even tell what some of the drawings were, and the toys . . . well, I couldn't remember who gave them to me or I didn't ever want them anyway.'

'Julie, what did you want to take with you but you couldn't and it was very hard to say goodbye to?'

She hardly waited for me to finish my question before she blurted out, 'My friends'.

'Tell me about them', I asked gently.

The descriptions of about four people followed.

'Were they sad when you went away?'

'Yes, my neighbour cried — that is the old lady — and my friend made me promise not to forget her.'

'Do you sometimes still feel sad when you think of your friends and where you used to live?'

'Of course', Julie said, 'but I think that I'm going to like it here'.

'Have you made new friends?'

'Yes, one so far.'

I thanked Julie for sharing her story. 'We are so glad to have you with us. I hope you count us as your friends and may there be lots of souvenirs of events to take with you whenever you leave.' She joined the rest of the children.

I continued, 'I was a person who went away. Yes, as part of my work before I moved to this city, I would have to go away quite a lot. On one particular occasion, I was to be away for five weeks. There was a special friend who felt sad that I was going away. Even though I was coming back in five weeks, to him it seemed a very long time. My special friend's name is Nathan and at the time he was five. We were really very good friends. I had met Nathan at church with his Mum and Dad. On that day, I was a visitor. Nathan's job, according to him, was to stand at the front door of the church, a little bit along from the minister, and chat with the folk as they came out. So, on this day, as it was my turn to shake hands with the congregation, right beside me I discovered I had a helper. When just about everyone had gone, we had a particularly long chat. Nathan told me about his family, his house, and about how good his mum was as a typist and would I like to come home for dinner.

'Well, because of that one meeting, I did visit Nathan's house and his mum became one of the people who helped me with typing. Of course, this meant many subsequent visits to Nathan's house.

'The day before I was to go away, I stopped by to say good-byes. At the door, Nathan had a present for me. "It's for you." He beamed as if he was giving me a priceless art treasure. The wrapping paper was totally covered with sticky tape. "I wrapped it myself", he beamed, "and I hope you don't have to rip the paper". Very carefully, I undid one corner of the wrapping. After lots and lots of unwrapping, my hand found a soft tissue ball in the centre of the package. So this was the gift. I unfolded the tissue wrapping. Guess what it was!'

I immediately delved into my pocket. Slowly I withdrew my hand and held at the tips of my fingers, a tiny porcelain elephant. Yes, this was Nathan's present — an elephant, the tiniest I've ever seen.

'As I held his gift in the palm of my hand, I said, "Thank you very much, Nathan, it's a beautiful present". He said, "It's to take with you, it's small, you see, so you can put it in your pocket". I just kept admiring it and Nathan watched me ever so intently, as if expecting me to say something more. For a moment, I thought perhaps I hadn't said thank you in the right way. Finally, Nathan spoke:

"Pauline, do you know what's special about elephants?" He seemed to want me to say something particular and I didn't know what.'

I directed a question to the children. 'Do you know what's special about elephants?' It wasn't long before one said, 'They never forget'. 'Yes, elephants never forget, but I forgot and Nathan wasn't very impressed. He said to me, rather peeved, "Elephants never forget". All of a sudden, I guessed why Nathan had chosen the elephant for a present. When I told him, he seemed delighted that I had 'caught on' at last. "Well, Pauline, why did I choose an elephant?" "You gave me this because you're not going to forget me when I go away." And I remember smiling, rather pleased now I understood. But Nathan frowned and looked a little sad. "No, that's not the reason, Pauline. I gave you the elephant because when you go away, I don't want you to forget me."

I paused at that point and repeated aloud Nathan's words. 'Nathan was a very good friend, wasn't he?' The children nodded vigorously. 'I still carry this little elephant, sometimes in my pocket, at other times in my handbag and I think of Nathan and our special friendship. It is a friendship that lasts, and Nathan was very serious about being my friend even when I was away.

'At some time or other, we are all people who go away from those we love and from those who love us. What is important is not so much giving a present so that people will remember you, but taking with you in your heart the gifts of friendship, and leaving behind you in their hearts memories of your own love and care through the way that you have played, and worked, and just been you.

'Saying good-bye is a part of everyone's life, and although we say good-bye to people, we do not say good-bye to their love. In fact, we can always take with us the most valuable things.

'There is someone else who had to say good-bye and who went away from those he loved very much. His name was Jesus. On the night before he died, he had a special meal with his best friends, his twelve disciples. He was feeling very sad about leaving them. It was important that he go away, because not only did he love those twelve disciples, he loved everybody.

'So that everyone — men, women and children — might know God's love and his forgiveness, and feel that he was their friend always, Jesus had to go away to die on the cross and suffer for us and rise again. Of course, he knew all this ahead of time and so he prepared a special going away. The meal was called the Passover Meal, and the bread and wine on the table was there for every Passover Meal. But what made this time very different was what Jesus did with the bread and the wine.'

Then I walked over to the Communion Table, and unveiled the bread and the wine prepared for communion later in the service. 'Jesus broke the bread' (I followed these words with that same action) 'and he said, "This is my body. It is broken for you. Eat this in memory of me". Then the disciples each took a piece of bread and ate it.'

I went on to explain the words of Jesus when he held the cup and drank at that very special meal. When I replaced the cup, I returned the porcelain elephant to my hand. 'Nathan's words remind me of those words of Jesus. They are words that you will hear again later in this service. But there is far more in the meaning of this meal and also in the little elephant than just remembering. When this family takes part in sharing the bread and the wine today, we not only remember Jesus and his words, but we know this is an occasion when he is especially present with us. He gave his life for us and now he lives to give us strength. We thank him for his promise that he is with us always.' I replaced the cloth on the Communion Table and turned to the children. 'We are so glad you can be with us, particularly today when we share in this special meal that we call a sacrament.'

Before the children returned to sit with the rest of the congregation, I prayed, asking that God might help us in all our good-byes and hellos, and that we might help other newcomers feel welcome and comfortable; that we might not forget the kindness and love of others.

THE SETTING

We are living in a very mobile society. Once upon a time, you bought a house and there you stayed with your family for many years. Of course, there were certain occupations which required regular moves but these were in the minority. That is not so today. It is not uncommon for families to make two or three moves in the span of a generation. Children and adults alike face many sad good-byes and traumatic hellos. In fact, within the members of every local church, this is the case. Another kind of 'hello' and 'good-bye' affects many children in our community, and whether we accept it or not, it includes our local church.

I was very aware that in recent months two families within this congregation experienced the sadness of a dad going away and not coming back. Going to church was a battle with shame and aloneness, but the mums with their children kept coming. Divorce and separation regretfully are a fact of life. The broken and bruised victims are more often the children. It was particularly important to me that the children who faced this trauma were affirmed and supported when they came to church. One of the most practical healing potions is to enable children and parents to talk about these experiences. Approaching the subject as I did, I hoped this would lead to conversation between parents and children in their homes after the service, or at appropriate moments in the following days.

Many churches are involved in the ministry of refugee settlement. The plight of the Indo-Chinese refugees has been put before every congregation. Some worship with us; many certainly share our faith, and their children sit beside our children at the local schools. To my mind 'talking about when people go away' invited the inclusion of these people and their stories. In so many ways, they were still strangers in a strange land. This was an opportunity to enable these people to tell their own story and to bring their faith and witness into our midst. No longer need they be faces staring at us from posters on walls, but warm human beings in our midst, with gifts to bring, but needing fellowship and family in their new home.

Having a reference point of stability and a source of reliable relationships is of great comfort to the person who moves to a new place. To my mind, the Christian church could provide this, and wherever our goings away take us, to be sure there is a Christian flock meeting not too far distant. Of course, it is sad to say good-bye to those in our church family, but in the new country or the new neighbourhood, by the grace of God, there will be another church family who will be happy to welcome us, and where new experiences and opportunities are waiting.

RESOURCING THE WORKSHOP

This service was for one of the families present, the last Sunday they would be spending in fellowship with us. Just days before, Dad received a promotion, which meant a move interstate. The family was prominent in leadership of the church and their contribution would be sadly missed. Before the prayers of intercession, the family received the special thanks and the blessing of everyone present, in all the new things they faced. Before the congregation emerged, they were invited to stand with me at the door at the close of the service, so that every member of the congregation had an opportunity to say good-bye. When the time came for the Communion elements to be served, this family of five came forward to assist. It seemed a beautiful gesture for them to minister to their congregation in this way, on their last Sunday.

MAKE-BELIEVE SURVIVAL KIT

I held an envelope in my hand and I asked the congregation to pretend that it was a survival kit. It was interwoven into the sermon in this way. 'If I had an opportunity to prepare a survival kit for each of you, it would contain these things.' Out of the envelope, I took a small round yellow sticker on which was painted a 'Smiley' face. 'Your survival kit must contain this. Let it stand for joy. You need never leave that behind.'

The second thing I drew from the envelope was another sticker but this time in the shape of a Bible, the sort you buy as Sunday school prizes at Christian bookshops. I made a point of describing what I was holding for the sake of those in the back pews. 'The word of God lasts forever. It will challenge and comfort you wherever you go, and however difficult the journey is.'

The third item was a small piece of paper on the top of which was written 'Dear God'. 'There is room on this to write a prayer or a promise to God. We must commit our lives to something and someone.'

The last item was a pipe cleaner. As I held this in my fingers and reflected, I slowly twisted it into different shapes. 'As you live, may you always be ready to move. May your spirit be open to change and may it be open to the needs of those around you.'

I replaced all the items in the envelope and concluded, 'May this be the Survival Kit for all of us'.

MEET OUR VIETNAMESE FRIENDS

The first part of the sermon was given over to an interview with two Vietnamese boys in their late teens. They shared the struggle and pain of their journey to freedom; the sadness of living away from members of their family and the experience of building a new life in a different culture.

Each brought with him a poem he had composed. Minh read his at the close of the interview:

> Sadness is living without a family;
> Sadness is living without the truth;
> Sadness is living without much enjoyment;
> Sadness is living without love;
> Sadness is living without friends;
> Sadness is not being well-educated;
> Sadness is living without the prospect of a good future;
> Sadness is living away from your own family.
>
> Used with permission of Quoc Minh Phu

This one I read following the 'Survival Kit' reflection:

> I need
>
> I need a purer life;
> I need a kinder heart;
> I need help to live and love and work;
> I need a stronger will;
> I need harmony;
> I need strength;
> I need purer thoughts.
>
> Used with permission of Quoc Tru Minh.

Chapter 13

Talking about feeling quiet

I held high the sticky-taped gift box. I wanted not only the children who were close to me, but all the congregation to see. 'Inside this box is something that every visitor to my house sees. It sits in a very important place in my lounge-room. I've wrapped it especially for this morning, but this is just how the sales lady packaged it at the airport gift shop. Of all the wonderful things that I saw in that shop, I loved this the best for so many reasons.' I then turned my attention specifically to the children. 'I thought that you might like to unwrap it for everyone', and I invited two of the children to do just this.

I didn't say anything as they carefully performed the unveiling ceremony. Everyone waited, quietly and expectantly. The tissue paper drifted to the floor. A simultaneous 'aahh' of pleasure burst softly from the children who watched. A hand-crafted and painted, wooden model of a church was now displayed for everyone to see. The two helpers moved along the rows of children with the model and then down the aisle of the church. A closer look was very important, I thought. Features like the tiny gold bell in the steeple, the arched brown doors, the stained glass windows and the model trees and shrubs of the church's garden were delicately made, and could only be seen at close distance. The children's eyes beamed. The little brown church was as delightful in its appearance to them as it was to me. From the twinkles and lighted faces of the adults, they obviously felt the same way.

The children returned the little church to me, and I held it high as I spoke. 'This little church had some important things to say to me that day I found it on the shop display shelf. Sometimes as I gaze at it, there in my lounge-room, it speaks to me again. What about I wonder?' The children looked very quizzical. I had chosen to use this model church to recall some memories and truths that were an important part of the spiritual journey of everyone in the congregation. I felt confident that the children would relate to this concept if they could focus on an object of interest. Indeed, the little church seemed to have an aura of enchantment for them. 'Will you listen for the voices with me today?'

'There is something that I haven't shown you yet about this little church. Listen!' I turned the small metal handle that protruded from the rear of the church. At first, no sound, then single notes of music, bell-like in their sound, filled the silence. They made a tune. Children strained to identify this song. The adults were exchanging smiles, and mouthing the words. Oh yes, they knew the melody! Several called out softly the name of the song. I turned to the children. 'You may never have heard it before, but your parents and friends remember it.' It had not been sung for many years in this church. I began to sing the words as I continued turning the handle:

'O, come to the church in the wildwood;
O, come to the church in the dale;
The spot is so dear to my childhood;
O, come to the church in the vale.'

I paused. 'Will you listen for the voices with me as I play this song?' So I turned the handle sufficient times for one chorus to tinkle.

'Do you know the voices I hear? I hear my own voice singing that song when I was very small. It was one of the favourite songs in the church that I attended as a little girl. I used to think that I was singing about my church. It was small, its wood was brown and, yes, my church was in the country too. But we would sing many other songs and how I loved singing with everyone! Oh, sometimes the songs seemed a little slow and hard to understand, but the singing always seemed very important to everyone. I would sing along too. Always, they were songs about God's people and Jesus' love for us.

'Some days when I'm driving in my car I start to sing.' At that point, I broke into song; two lines of 'Jesus keep me near the cross' and then two lines of 'Trust and obey', no music accompaniment, just my voice keeping as close to the traditional beat as I could. I smiled at the children and gestured, 'It's as if the words of those hymns are printed deep inside me. When I sing them, I hear other people singing too. People who encouraged me to sing with them in that little brown church; people who loved God, and people whose faces and smiles are like pictures in my mind'. I recalled the names and faces of many who were in that congregation; I described idiosyncrasies and lovable qualities.

I picked up the church. 'Listen for another voice.' I turned the handle. Everyone was so still, listening. The music box notes tinkled:

'O, come to the church in the wildwood;
O, come to the church in the dale;
No spot is so dear to my childhood;
As the little brown church in the vale.

'Do you know what I hear? It's the voice of a special friend. Miss Best was her name. She was an old lady who never missed coming to church. She was my Sunday school teacher, too. Every Sunday, she would call out my name and give my hand a gentle squeeze when I arrived. When I was away, she would ask about my health. Sometimes in church, she would turn to give me a smile or a nod. It always seemed to be at those times when I felt the time was going a little too slowly, just sitting there. Miss Best seemed to know my thoughts and always I was sure she understood. She loved me as a special friend and helped me to feel very sure that Jesus loved me and wanted me in his family.' I asked the children, 'Who's got a friend like Miss Best here today?' Three or four hands eagerly indicated 'Yes'.

'Will you listen for the third voice with me? It's the most important of all.' One more time, I turned the handle for the little church to play 'O come to the church in the wildwood'. After one chorus, I stopped and this time I said nothing for several seconds. I just stood with the little church in my hands as if I was listening and hearing. Everyone was listening in the stillness, but there was only silence. When I spoke, though, it was loud enough for folk to hear but it was a hushed whisper tone. 'That voice is the most powerful of all. It is the one I love the most. I call it the voice of the "quiet feeling, peaceful inside". It is the voice of God when he comes to us in the silence. His voice is still and small. Many times, when I sat in church as a small child, it was just like it is now — very still and quiet. I would look around and see people praying. I would play softly with my purse or hymn book, perhaps daydream a little, but there were other times when I found myself thinking about God and Jesus.

'I described the feeling of talking to God in these quiet times, not aloud, but inside, from my heart. 'It was my silent prayer, and as I prayed, I felt very sure that God was calling me to be one of Jesus' friends and to follow Jesus' way of caring for people and loving them. I began to enjoy the times of stillness and silence. They were very special when I felt him within me, with the people who sat all around me. God wants you to know that calm and quiet feeling inside. He wants you to be ready for those times when he will speak to you. That "quiet feeling, peaceful inside" is something everybody needs for all their lives. Here in the family of Jesus, we must help others to be calm and peaceful inside.'

At that point, I picked up my guitar, strummed softly, and began to sing:

'Quiet feeling, peaceful inside,
That's what I feel just now.
I whisper to God all the things in my heart,
Quiet feeling, peaceful inside.

Quiet feeling, peaceful inside,
That's what I feel in my heart,
God knows me, he cares and he understands;
Quiet feeling, peaceful inside.

At the conclusion of the song, I announced a time of silent prayer and introduced it in this way: 'All the voices I have shared with you are ways in which God has spoken to me in my life. Children, in the silence I would like you to think of a person, more than one if you like, who is special to you in the way Miss Best was to me; or there may be a song that we sing that you love for a particular reason; or a place that you visit or are part of that is also very special. I want you to picture them in your minds — the face, the name.' Then I looked at the adults. 'Many of you have had a similar journey to me and as I played this tune and shared the voices of my childhood, I am sure people, places and tunes filled some of those memory pockets. In the silence and as a prayer, I invite all of you to call out the name of a person, the title of that hymn or song, you may even like to sing one or two lines, the name of your church. That's all you need to say, and just where you are. If two or three speak at the same time, that doesn't matter. Children, you are especially invited to take part. Let us, as a family, thank God for the friends, songs and places that have helped and healed us and, in a way beyond our understanding, bring us together here.'

Many of the children participated. After a little while, I turned the handle of the little church again. 'O, come to the church in the wildwood' blended with our prayers.

THE SETTING

This was a case of introducing a subject to the children that I was still learning about myself. Let me explain. Some years ago, I spent a great deal of time organising camps for primary school children and high schoolers on behalf of the church. I prided myself on combining exciting programs and exciting team leaders with a holiday atmosphere, very colourful, very complex and very stimulating. Truly, it was a psychedelic mix.

One regular event at every one of these camps began to trouble me. At the first mealtime, I would request all those children who had brought with them medications of any kind to come and see me after the meal, with their bottles, etc. Always, a great long line of children responded, sometimes 40% of the total number of campers. Those who had coughs, colds and allergies didn't unnerve me so much as those who handed to me valium or another of the great variety of tranquilisers from the bottomless pit of medicinal panacea. Often wrapped around the bottle of tablets was a little note from Mum or Dad which began, 'Tim is hyperactive . . . '

'Were these camping experiences helping these children be less hyperactive?' nagged at my confidence in what I had organised. Was it a good thing that the only times the children were quiet and peaceful was when they dropped from exhaustion, or were forced to appear so in a didactic teaching situation.

No, I was convinced that this was in no way healing for children, and instinctively began to adapt my camping programs to provide for some winding-down experiences.

One particular ritual introduced at the end of the day brought quietness and peace to us all. My program sequence used to read:

supper, devotions, walk, bedtime. I re-slotted devotions between the walk and bedtime, and I planned the setting in this way: in every large group of children who came to camp, there was always half a dozen who seemed to stand out because of the trouble they caused and for the riotous nature of their personality. These same children also had very lovable qualities and enormous potential for leadership and responsibility. I enlisted these children to help me with the evening devotions.

While the main body of the camp was out for their evening walk, we worked feverishly to change one half of the dining hall into a sanctuary. Cardboard boxes with one or two blankets became an altar, seats and cushions were arranged in a half circle, posters were straightened, floors were swept and lights were dimmed. The last act of interior decorating was coveted by all the children. That was the lighting of the candles. Usually, we added a candle for each day passed at the camp. It was as if they sensed a spirit of hallowedness in the arranging and lighting of these candles. As they shone in the dim light, so did the faces of these children.

I was very direct in my instructions to this small team. They were to hush, in a gentle way, the children as they came back from their walk and they were to encourage throughout the devotions a quiet, peaceful feeling. Never a moment of hesitation or misunderstanding occurred between us. Instinctively, these children, often classed as hyperactive nuisances, knew what I was on about.

A final touch before the children arrived was soft music, usually a prayer chorus provided by an acoustic guitar and soft singing. All who entered were instantly mellowed by the singing and the special touches to the *décor*.

There followed a story from the Bible, told without flip-chart or flannel graph, and then I would reflect on the day's events, the glad and the sad. We closed with a prayer.

I was most nervous about this prayer time. My intention was to invite children to offer a sentence aloud. I expected giggles and nudges at the very least; at the worst, the prayer could turn into the raucous conversation of many children. However, this was not the case. The children seemed to move naturally in the spirit of this prayer time. I tried to help them by a gentle explanation and some suggestions that might guide their thoughts.

I would say something along these lines: 'It may happen that two or three of you begin your sentence at the same time, but this is all right, for God will hear you all. It may be that in the silence, you will want to laugh or whisper to your neighbour, for sometimes silence make us uncomfortable. I understand that and if you feel that you must, do it as quietly as you can. Remember to be considerate of those near you. Today, let us think about the friends we have made, the things we have done, the world in which we live, and the people who love us and who need our love. I will begin with a sentence "Let us all pray in the quietness". I would close the prayer with the same chorus that had opened the devotional time.

These ten minutes at the close of each day gave some 'difficult' children a new dimension to their lives. I dare say it was a healing experience for all the other children also.

There was now an extra spirit alive and well in the camping program; this was the calm and quiet spirit. The children were getting in touch with the still, small voice of God inside each one of them. By the way, so was the leader.

I have set down so much detail for you because I want to provide evidence of a very important truth. It is this: children who are out of touch with their inner spirit will have very little chance of ever getting in touch later in life. If given the opportunity, however, children will open themselves to this spirit. It is the spirit of Jesus and it dwells within our children in a way that is not characteristic of adults.

A renowned psychologist, Dorothy Cohen, whose work has for many years often been underestimated and misunderstood, is now recognised as having uncovered some startling observations in relation to the effects overstimulation has on children. Before her death, she played a leading role in analysing the effects that fast moving television programs such as 'Sesame Street' have on the personalities of children, over a period of time. Her findings, which have since been supported by many psychologists and researchers in the Western World are these, that the continued bombardment of fast-moving images and information that dominates television and radio programming and education methods is winding our children up like a clock-work spring. Although producing very literate children, this has resulted in frenetic behaviour patterns in them.

What this means is that although children can read the words and recite the numbers, when it comes to taking part in a person-to-person conversation for any length of time, or entertaining themselves, or feeling comfortable when they are not being entertained, it is simply not achievable for them. Our children are busy at aimless activity. The solution is not to abandon such programs and methods but rather provide a counter-balance for our children. We need to help them to wind-down, be still, in as natural a way as they apply themselves to business.

I was certain that this time with the children would speak to the heart of many adults. Hyperactivity may not be a term ascribed to adults, but Australians over eighteen are certainly ardent consumers of anti-depressants, tranquilisers and the like. More leisure time, better working conditions, increased opportunities to travel the world, retirement at an earlier age, driving in air-conditioned cars . . . have not resulted in relaxed and contented Australians living with purpose and meaning.

Nervous breakdowns, ulcers, hypertension, destructive social behaviour are the symptoms of people not at peace with themselves, a people without calm at their centre, whose storms of life rage within.

I see the Christian church as playing a very important role in helping children and their parents understand and get in touch with this quiet spirit that is so important to the health of our mental, physical and spiritual being.

In particular, I see the worship gathering as one of the special times and places for babies and small children to be encouraged to feel calm and to enjoy moments of stillness. The awe, wonder and spirit of reverence that fill segments of our worship can be a healing balm for our children. In the silence, we trust that God will speak to them. In the calm, their hearts will whisper to God.

Earlier, I mentioned that this was a subject which I was still in the process of understanding. Living with tension, pressure, and constant change sometimes drowns that still small voice. This particular Sunday, as I talked with the children, my own spirit was open and attentive to the presence of God.

RESOURCING THE WORSHIP

This was one occasion when I saw no difficulty in tying a close connection between my time with the children and the remainder of the liturgy. In fact I saw the childrens address and the sermon as overlapping and complementing each other. I guess that is desirable for every church worship service, but for me, this seemed to be more attainable on this day.

PRESENTING THE BIBLE PASSAGES

Much time and enthusiasm was spent in preparation of the lessons of the day. Two passages in particular were of great impact in the flow of the liturgy:

Mark 4: 35-41 — The calming of the storm.

This story was prepared in two rehearsals by two classes as part of the Sunday school lesson time. It came immediately prior to my time with the children.

It was the small children, a dozen in number, who presented the 'calming of the storm' to the rhythm of instrumental folk music and a narrator. The communion rail became the confines of a boat. Blue cellophane streamers clutched in tiny hands were waves that swept over the disciples. This segment lasted two minutes and culminated with all the children in a freeze position as the words 'peace, be still' echoed throughout the church.

Psalm 31 — A prayer of trust in God.

I particularly asked one of the older men in the congregation to read this. His voice was cracked yet very dramatic and that was the sort of voice I hoped for. Classical music played softly behind his reading, and filled pauses that he had rehearsed at appropriate points in the psalm.

The reading was set in this context: I asked the congregation to feel into the mood of this psalm and to reflect upon its meaning for their own lives. I added that there would be a time of silence following this psalm where together we would ask God to calm the storms that rage within us, and drive away the enemies within. This silence was concluded by the Lord's prayer.

SERMON

The text was John 14:27 — 'Let not your hearts be troubled, neither let them be afraid'.

I drew on incidents with children and young people who, in the tempestuousness of their own lives, had sought desperately for a feeling of inner calm, and a sense of inner meaning for their lives. Towards the close, I picked up the little church once more and spoke about the comforting embrace of the love of Jesus within his family. I reminded the congregation that the time to enable our children and little ones to find the calm and quiet spirit was now, and one of the most powerful environments was here, within this body of people. Within this challenge was an indirect warning that the 'peace, be still' that Jesus desires for us comes from within and can only be encouraged from without. This must not be confused with a silence that is cold, imposing and stifling.

BENEDICTION

With a special effort, I learned in paraphrase fashion, John 14:27-31. Introduced by 'Hear the words of Jesus', this was the benedictory blessing before a threefold 'Amen'.

Chapter 14

Principles to go with

Who bakes the best cake? Some bake by following a recipe diligently; all the ingredients are carefully weighed and blended with meticulous allegiance to what the book says. Others bake according to what they feel to be 'just right'. 'A little bit of this and some of that should do it' is the attitude that stirs the mix. Which cakes turns out to be the best? Sometimes it is the cake baked *à la recipe*, other times it will be the cake baked according to intuitive guess work. But always the proof of the pudding is in the eating, not in the recipe. The 'principles to go with' align closely with this analogy.

You may follow all of them to the letter, but still the segment may come unstuck. On other occasions, you will by-pass the rules, take what seems a few too many risks, but yet your time with the children is a moving and powerful experience that lifts the whole service of worship.

There were no rules when we began sharing this way with children in the worship hour. What follows are principles that have evolved through time and varied experiences that have wrought failures as well as successes. For us, they are tried and tested. I am sure as we continue to delve into this integral part of the worship life of the church, the list will grow. There will be some to adapt and more to add. May they be a recipe which inspires your own creativity, builds a confidence in your intuitive judgment and enables you to keep in tune with the childlike spirit within!

WHAT'S YOURS IS THEIRS

The concerns and cares that you have are, more often than not, those of the children in your life and in your church. They see the same world as you do; they feel some of the pain you feel; they share many of the same joys. Instinctively, they desire to walk with you and share it all. Although the children will sometimes perceive and interpret life differently, be sure that what is and has been important to you in your life, is a rich resource for 'Talking about Something Important'.

WHAT'S THEIRS IS YOURS

Take time to chat with children about their lives, their friends, their hobbies, their hopes, their dreams. These will be shared with you unsparingly if they sense you like to be with them.

Be willing to talk about your life and your experiences. You will not have to learn a new language, or dress in the latest trends. *You may worry about the age difference and the barrier in communication that this may mean; the children won't concern themselves with either!*

NO VISUALS, NO WORRIES — NO PLAY, NO PANIC

If a flannel graph or chalk board is not integral to this time with the children, then don't use one. If you're not a ventriloquist, don't feel pressed to try. These may, at times, provide the icing on the cake for Christian education settings, but they often confuse the flow of the worship or result in 'sit and be entertained' situations. However, do not hesitate to seek out an object, a picture or a painting which can become a symbol of meaning enabling you to tell your story, or provide a springboard for discussion or reflection. Such simple objects were the tools that Jesus used, to tell the parables. However, for children, talking about something important is also talking with someone important to them. Be the believable, human person, rather than 'larger than life' or 'holier than life'.

RESTFUL RATHER THAN RIOTOUS

With your own attitude and gestures, encourage the children to feel comfortable with a restful and quiet spirit. However, we must not confuse this quiet spirit with dull and boring discourse. Neither a child nor an adult can feel at peace in this atmosphere. When there's opportunity for laughter and energetic participation, go to it! The warning is to find a balance and enable the children to wind down and listen to that still small voice within.

AFIX A MORAL — LOSE SOME MEANING

For some of the most important issues of life, there are no easy answers. That is a more powerful and helpful message than moralising and tying all the loose ends in a neat bow. Life is not like that and be sure that the children will soon know it!

METHOD MAKETH THE MODEL

How you talk with the children and what you talk about will model for the parents, and in fact the whole congregation, new possibilities for relationships with the children among their number. You will be giving them an invaluable gift.

NOT 'ADULTS ONLY' OR 'CHILDREN ONLY'

Although 'Talking about Something Important' is prepared with children and their lives especially in mind, it should not exclude adults. In the same way, this time should not be seen as if it is an optional insert in an otherwise 'Adults Only' worship. To provide connecting links between this time and the prayers, sermon and readings is a sign to children that they are welcome throughout the entire liturgy.

CHILDREN TO BE SEEN AND HEARD

One of the gifts children bring us is their physical beauty. It is not a beauty they are aware of; but certainly, adults notice it and find it heartening and healing. When you speak to a child, have him or her at your level, and share your microphone with them. This may mean the addition of a box, bench or chair to that part of the sanctuary. To take the opinions and presence of the children seriously is to enable them to be seen and heard.

DON'T DISAPPEAR

Sometimes, it is tempting to sit on the floor with the children and chat with them there. For the adults, this means long minutes of straining to hear the muffled conversation. As for seeing what is happening, this is out of the question. Don't cut the adults off. More often than not, they want to be involved.

IN CONCLUSION

When all else fails, children will value this principle more than any other. Let them see that you love them and allow them to love you!

From the children in your church . . .

1. We belong to you, we're members of this family.
   We are part of you, doesn't it show?
   We can be a help to you, if you'll only let us.
   Will you help us as we grow?
   Will you share just what you know?

2. We like to talk with you, if you'll only listen.
   We will work with you, if you'll give us jobs.
   We'd like to sit with you, and sometimes hold your hand.
   Will you take us where you go?
   Will you wait for us when we're slow?

3. We love playing, will you come and join us?
   We love singing, won't you sing our songs?
   We're very good at parties, let's have one together.
   All these things you and I can do.
   I can be a good friend to you.

4. We don't understand all you say or do.
   But, if you make us welcome, we'll stay with you.
   We belong to you, not just when we're older.
   Though we're young, we can make a start.
   There's room for us to play our part.

About the authors

Stan Stewart started writing about children and the church in 1975. In that year, he was employed by the Australian Council of Christian Education to research trends in childrens ministry in the Australian church. That work led the Council to publish Stan's first two books *The Church's Ministry with Children Report* and *The Church's Ministry with Children Ideas Catalogue*.

In 1978, Stan teamed with the American Christian educator, Dennis Benson, to write a book for the Year of the Child. This book published by Abingdon Press (Nashville) is titled *The Ministry of the Child*.

Over recent years, Stan has led workshops throughout Australia and New Zealand on the topic of children in the church. He has been employed on a half-time basis by the Ringwood (Victoria) Parish of the Uniting Church.

Pauline Hubner was heavily involved in childrens ministry in her work as Director of Childrens Camping for the Department of Christian Education of the Queensland Methodist Church. During this period, she developed sets of camp studies and devotional materials which still have wide currency. She continued her interest at another level, as Director of the Christian Television Association of New South Wales, in which capacity, she gave special attention to the development of television spots and programs for children. She remains much in demand as a workshop leader and presenter, on special occasions where children are in prominence.

Pauline and Stan have worked together on a number of projects. They developed a series of half-hour childrens television programs, which screen in several Australian states under the title 'A People to Belong To'. In 1979 and again in 1980, they were employed by the United Methodist Church in the United States of America to lead workshops on childrens ministry.

This book is the third writing project by Pauline and Stan. In 1979, they wrote *Worship Is for All Ages* published by the Joint Board of Christian Education.

In 1980, they wrote *Building your Church as a People to Belong to*, to be published in 1982 by Abingdon Press, Nashville.